P.E.P.
THE SEVEN P'S TO POSITIVELY ENHANCE PERFORMANCE

BY
RICH RUFFALO
WITH MIKE MORETTI

HARA
PUBLISHING
Seattle, Washington

Published by
Hara Publishing
P.O. Box 19732
Seattle, WA 98109
(425) 775-7868

First Printing, February, 1996
Second Printing, July, 1997
Third Printing, February, 1998
Fourth Printing, April, 1998
Fifth Printing, March, 1999
Sixth Printing, August, 2001

Fifty thousand copies in print worldwide.

ISBN: 1-883697-23-9
Library of Congress Number: 96-77150

Manufactured in the United States
12 11 10 9 8 7

Editor: Vicki McCown
Cover Design: Ron de Wilde
Desktop Publishing: Shael Anderson

DEDICATION

To my wife, Dianne
whose love has enriched my life
beyond measure and to
my daughter, Sara
our special gift.

To my wife's family and my family,
especially my father, Joseph, and
my mother, Rose Ruffalo,
who taught me to never say no
when it comes to helping people.

To Michael A. Lally,
Superintendent of Schools,
Belleville, New Jersey,
for his belief in me, and to
the Administration and
the Belleville Board of Education,
for supporting his decision.

To all people who face personal adversity,
to assure them that they can slay
their personal Goliaths.

ACKNOWLEDGMENTS

Special thanks to:

Mike Moretti, who for over thirty years has been my dear friend and has helped me immeasurably throughout this project.

My former coach, the late Dr. George Horn of Montclair State University, and all my coaches who have guided me over the years.

Sheryn Hara and her staff for all of their assistance in helping this book come to fruition.

A butterfly is a caterpillar
with the courage to change.

"Rich Ruffalo is an international spokesperson for the campaign for Victory Over Violence, helping victims and survivors of any form of violence rise from tragedy to triumph."

Fred "V-Man" Watson
International founder of Victory
Over Violence campaign

TABLE OF CONTENTS

PROLOGUE

"Life is like a book with many different chapters. Some tell of tragedy, others of triumph. Some chapters are dull and ordinary, others intense and exciting. The key to being a success in life is to never stop on a difficult page, to never quit on a tough chapter. Champions have the courage to keep turning the pages because they know a better chapter lies ahead."

—Rich Ruffalo

Rich Ruffalo is a champion. His road to personal and professional success has been a difficult one, however, and more than once he contemplated ending the journey altogether. Instead, he kept turning the page, moving on to the next chapter in his life, and ultimately to the tremendous rewards he now enjoys.

Rich suffers from retinitis pigmentosa, a degenerative disease which eventually robbed him of his eyesight as a young adult. A teacher, coach, and world class athlete, Rich thought being blind meant he'd never live a life of independence and accomplishment. Anger, despair, and frustration sent him into downward spiral until one important day when he found a way to turn it all around.

Since that day, Rich has enjoyed many hard-won triumphs. He has competed for the U.S. as a member of the United States Association for Blind Athletes in a number of international track and field events, including the 1988 Paralympics in Seoul, South Korea, where he won a gold medal. He has also been recognized as one of the nation's outstanding teachers, receiving the unprecedented double honor as the "Most Outstanding Teacher" and "Coach of the Year" for 1995 at the American Teachers Awards, sponsored by Walt Disney Company and McDonald's.

Although Rich continues to do what he loves most—teaching and coaching kids—he also has become a charismatic motivational speaker. He addresses groups all around the country, from Boy Scout troops to Fortune 500 executives, sharing his insight on how to meet and triumph over adversity. At a time when so many professional athletes decline to be a positive role model, Rich embraces that role and its responsibility. He is uniquely qualified to inspire his fellow man for his story is truly inspirational.

In *P.E.P. - The Seven P's to Positively Enhance Performance*, Ruffalo takes the reader down the same road he had to travel to build character, develop self-esteem, and achieve success. It is a journey well worth taking.

About the Coauthor

Mike Moretti has had a long and distinguished career as a sports journalist, including the distinction of being named the New Jersey "Sportswriter of the Year" for 1995-96. His column can be found in *The Star-Ledger* of Newark, N.J., one of the country's top newspapers.

Mike brings a unique perspective to this story, having known Rich Ruffalo on a personal basis for more than 30 years. He has personally witnessed Rich's metamorphosis from a lost and angry young man into one of the country's most honored citizens. Without his collaboration, Rich's story would still be waiting to be told.

CHAPTER ONE
"PLUMMET"

"You L-O-S-E when you Lack Of Self-Esteem, when you Lack Of Spiritual Enlightenment, when you lack Love Of Something Else much greater than yourself.

"You W-I-N when you do Whatever Is Necessary to use your intellect and turn your life around. You may then gain Lots Of Self-Esteem, Lots Of Spiritual Enlightenment and have a Love Of Something Else, leading to a W-I-N in the great game of life."

For some people, there is a need to plummet, to take a sharp and death-defying fall and be humbled before learning how to arise and straighten out their lives.

That's what happened to me. I was barely twenty years old when I knew I was losing my eyesight to the degenerative disease known as retinitis pigmentosa. I refused to believe it. I wasted valuable time just waiting for this   tragedy to unfold instead of preparing for the future. Each day I would check my eyes to evaluate how much less I could see from the day before, wishing away the inevitable and sinking deeper into despair

This denial and negative thinking only added to my plummet.

I finally hit rock bottom during my senior year of college when, while driving, I struck a little girl who was crossing the street on a dark, rainy night.

I had been clinging to my driver's license as my last lifeline to independence, as though it were proof that I couldn't really be going blind. But the accident confirmed it: I *was* going blind and there was nothing I could do about it. It was a bitter pill I had refused to swallow. In doing so, I created an even greater moral abyss for myself by dwelling on things negative to my body and soul.

Fortunately, the 12-year-old girl suffered only a broken arm, but I was left with a broken heart and shattered self-esteem. For the next several months, I suffered from flashbacks of the incident and from fits of depression. I had recurring nightmares about it: The sound of screeching brakes, the smell of burning rubber, the thud of the impact.

Still, I could not bring myself to give up my license

as I surely should have. Instead, I limited myself to driving as little as possible and only during the day.

My life began to fall apart as I spiraled downward into negativity and frustration. I became violent and self-destructive. I bitterly resented that my most prized posses-sion, my skill as a track and field athlete and enjoyment of participating in other sports, was being taken away by my failing eyesight.

I had thoughts of suicide and became abusive to my friends and family. I had unpredictable and savage outbursts fueled by heavy drinking and self-pity.

This was not the first time my physical frailties threatened my happiness. In fact, my intense bitterness was rooted in my memories of earlier health problems.

As a six-year-old I nearly died of a kidney disorder. I was housebound for six months while other kids in the neigh-borhood were playing outside, doing all the things I loved to do. I could see them, almost touch them, but I couldn't be one of them. I felt like a little lost puppy dog staring out the window every day, begging for a token of affection.

Even as a kid, my poor eyesight caused me problems. I was forced to wear cumbersome tortoise-shell spectacles that made me an obvious target for ridicule by my classmates and playmates. Many was the time I wished I could have perfect vision like the other kids.

As I grew older and stronger, I began to improve as an athlete. I was at my peak following my sophomore year of high school, sure that I could make the junior varsity basketball team at Bloomfield High. One day, while I was supposed to be babysitting my younger brother Robert, the neighborhood kids knocked on my door, asking me to play tackle football with them. I couldn't resist. I dropped off little Robert at a neighbor's house and took off with my friends. We had a fantastic game going until I made a tackle against the biggest kid on the field and broke my leg in seven places.

That cost me a spot on the basketball team. In fact, the leg never healed properly, throwing off my gait and making it even harder for me to succeed as an athlete. But all of these setbacks were minor compared to the physical disability I feared was inevitable: complete blindness.

When I graduated from Montclair State College with my degree in science education, I was immediately hired for my first teaching job at Monroe Street School in an urban suburb of Newark. It was one of the most tumbled-down areas in the state of New Jersey, and Monroe was a real-life blackboard jungle, the kind of place where teachers and students did battle on a daily basis.

Lots of kids in this school had knives, guns, num-chuck sticks, and almost any other weapon you could think of. When I took the job, I was only 21 years old, yet I would be teaching students in the seventh and eighth grade who were 17 years old!

Some of the kids I'll never forget. The looks on their faces are forever etched in my mind's eye. I'm sorry to say that I don't doubt that more than a few of them are in jail or dead from drugs or violence.

What went on at Monroe Street School on a daily basis was hard to believe. Incidents which would have been considered outrageous by most people were common every-day occurrences. Students stole a pocketbook from a female teacher, then proceeded to beat her over the head with it. A gang of boys jumped one of the male instructors. We teachers were always on our guard, looking over our shoulders, aware that we were constant targets for the students' anger and abuse.

As a man standing six-foot-two and weighing 215 pounds, I thought I could take care of myself. I was only kidding myself.

I was a rookie teacher, more than a little naive and full of ambition and noble thoughts. I thought I was going to change the world. And yet personally I was still going through my own troubles. My ebbing eyesight caused such frustration and anger, I was a powder keg ready to explode.

My new struggles as a teacher produced even more stress. I was teaching kids who didn't want to learn. I hated my job and that began to take its toll on me. After just one semester of teaching at Monroe Street School, I was run down and depressed. I'd go home on Friday night and drink for three straight days. I'd go to bed drunk, wake up with a hangover, and then start drinking again.

One of the worst kids in my class, Maurice, had a brother whom I heard had been stabbed. When I saw Maurice and asked him how he was doing, he shrugged and just kept on eating his potato chips and drinking his soda. He acted as if his brother were a bug that just got squashed on a windshield. That showed me how insensitive people became about life in the ghetto.

Another day, I told Ricky, also a tough guy, to sit down. He wouldn't budge. When I walked down the aisle between the old-fashioned desks, he put up his fists as if he were ready to punch me. In anger, I picked him up by his collar, all five-foot-six inches and 115 pounds of him, and shoved him up against the wall, holding him as high as I could.

As he dangled above me, he started to cry. His frightened pleas brought me back to reality and I realized what I was doing. If he had said the wrong thing, I would have dropped him and surely injured him.

It was the first time I lost control, but it wasn't the last. I was jumped from behind several times in those hallways. Once, four students surrounded me and told me they were going to whip my butt. Sure enough, when classes ended that day, they came right into my classroom. I was forced to defend myself, and summoned all the moves I remembered from watching professional wrestling on TV.

When the dust settled, they picked themselves up off the floor and meekly filed out of the classroom.

Yes, it was insane. But to ghetto kids who have to sometimes act like warriors, it was their way of staying sharp. To them it was a red badge of courage to say they got their behinds whipped by Mr. Ruffalo.

They started calling me "Mr. Ruff," but what they really meant was "Mr. Rough." They continued to think up ways in which they could take me on. This was the mid-1970s, and a lot of the kids were into Kung Fu and karate. Near the end of school one day, my "students" set me up for a fall.

One of the toughest youngsters gave me some back-talk. As I walked toward the end of his row, the kids suddenly moved their desks to box me into the rear corner of the classroom.

The entire room of 13 eighth-grade boys, kids ranging from 14 to 17 years of age, started attacking and beating me. I was literally fighting for my life. I knew I had to back up against the wall, because if they got me on the floor, I'd be done for.

They made the mistake of hitting me from so many sides at once, that I could still stand upright. They didn't all try to take me down from the same angle. I pushed and shoved my way out of the melee.

When I was finished, the 13 boys were strewn about the room. It had been a struggle for survival and I had no choice but to do what I did. Strangely, after that incident, I sensed a different kind of respect from the students.

I began to tire of breaking up classroom fights, an almost everyday occurrence. Assaults on the faculty continued. One female teacher was beaten over the head with a telephone and knocked unconscious. The beating led to a nervous breakdown. Another woman, the music teacher, was pushed down the stairs. She quit teaching. Monroe Street School was a terrible place to teach—or to try and get an education.

As I was walking down the stairs one day, the bell rang for lunch and a stampede was under way. Suddenly, I felt two hands on my back, trying to push me down the cement stairwell. I grabbed the railing in an effort to save myself and was able to turn around and see my attacker, who still had his arms extended in a pushing motion. He had a horrified look on his face because he had never expected me to brace myself and catch him in the act.

It was one of my own students, Tyrone. He was a short, squatty kid with a mouthful of purple bubble gum and a few teeth missing from that mouth. Tyrone's eyebrows were permanently knitted, giving him a perpetual frown to produce the meanest look possible. Every word I heard pass those lips was negative and biting. He was emotionless, no doubt one of the toughest nuts to crack in that school.

After grabbing him, I discreetly detained Tyrone and once the hallway was clear of students, gave him a short but effective "private" conference.

After that incident, I knew I had to get out of there. I was being destroyed emotionally and physically. I thought I had gone to college to become a teacher, not some boxing referee. I desperately wanted to make a change.

I'd go home, get drunk, get sick and then I'd cry. I just couldn't take it any more. The situation and my reaction to it was getting progressively worse and worse.

I had more unfortunate experiences in that one year than most teachers undergo in a lifetime. In retrospect, such experiences made me a better teacher and helped me to become successful. After such a brutal awakening in my chosen profession, I knew I could handle anything.

One of my eighth-grade girls, Patty, developed a crush on me. This was no normal student crush. Patty, who had long dark hair and wild brown eyes, would lay under the wheels of my car at the end of school each day so I wouldn't be able to pull out of the parking lot. Each afternoon, I had to get down on the ground and coax her to move.

I knew there was something misconnecting behind those wild eyes of hers. She would do anything to shock me, and when she did, those eyes only got wider.

As a rookie teacher, I had no idea what made her do the things she did. Looking back, I often wonder what her troubled eyes had seen. I have a better understanding now of the kind of background and negative influences that Patty, and others like her, were living through at home day after day.

In contrast to the students, I had my own ordered, stable lifestyle, a consistency they had never known. Those kids' lives might have been filled with fright, horror and shock. They probably had to desensitize themselves in order to survive, but the scars they suffered never truly healed.

Crazy, unprovoked incidents continued to unfold at Monroe Street School. In one occurrence, a student named Curtis, punched a female teacher in the face, just for fun.

Lenny, one of the biggest, toughest teachers, decided to take matters into his own hands so he kicked Curtis down three flights of stairs and rolled him out the front door of the school. On his discipline card, Lenny wrote that Curtis "...fell on my foot many times, in rapid succession, down the stairwell."

Curtis' mother came to school later that day for a conference with Lenny, and the two had a pleasant conversation. It turned out to be a fortunate thing that Lenny survived the conference with that woman. In the next day's newspaper, we all read that later in the afternoon, Curtis' mother had shot and killed her brother-in-law. She may even have had the murder weapon with her when she spoke with Lenny.

That was enough for him. He never touched another student. In fact, by the end of the school year, he had a teaching job lined up in another district.

Lenny was just the first to go. We were all jockeying for position to somehow get the hell out of there. The year I arrived at the school, 13 of the 36 teachers were in their first year. The turnover rate was tremendous.

I knew it wasn't the right way to teach. I'd visit my mother and she'd notice that my watch face was broken and ask me if I was fighting again. I'd tell her I smacked it into a locker by mistake.

Fortunately, a job opened up for me the next fall at Belleville High School. At the time I took the position, I thought I'd be teaching biology, in which I had majored. As it turned out, I had four courses to teach: three basic electricity classes, one electronics class, one environmental science and one biology class. That meant four different preps and a tremendous amount of work for me.

At that time, I was also studying for my graduate degree at Montclair State College. Being assigned to teach four brand new classes meant reading four different textbooks, making four sets of teaching notes and creating four sets of exams. Of course, all of this reading and studying was made even more difficult and time-consuming by my failing eyesight. And to top things off, I became the head coach of the cross country and track-and-field teams at the high school!

My first year of teaching at Belleville was intense. Adding stress to my life was my fear of losing my independence, mainly the ability to get around by myself, especially by car. I continued to deny my handicap since no doctor or ophthalmologist, or anyone in an official capacity, had ever correctly identified my problem. But I worried about it constantly.

What gave me solace that year was coaching. I loved working with the kids and watching them progress. I had always enjoyed that, being around people and helping them out. Coaching took my mind off the other pressures I had been under.

My eyesight was only getting worse and my night vision was terrible. My reading ability was decreasing and diminishing to where I could barely read the mail. I was really struggling to see things. I'd started to use subterfuge and all sorts of little tricks to try and hide it from my students.

However, kids can sense when you're putting them on. If you're not honest and up front with them, they'll tear your cover apart.

Because I still denied my failing eyesight, I had discipline problems with the students. They got away with all sorts of things and my reaction to their antics was not good. Out of the classroom I was still drinking a lot, even more than during my days at Monroe Street School.

Instead of drinking beer like most of my friends, I went over the edge and drank the hard stuff, usually bourbon. I could drink up to a dozen bourbons a night and really do some damage to myself. When I'd get drunk, I'd turn mean and nasty. It was my way of reacting to what I was going through.

I was overly sensitive and easily provoked. If someone said to me, "Rich, so-and-so over there is talking about you," I'd go over to that person and threaten to kill him. My friends thought it was funny to whip me into a lather. But it was a dangerous game, because when the alcohol went into my body, my frustration and anger could make me turn violent.

Those were the days when I started breaking doors. I'd rip them off the hinges and put my fist through them. I may not have been able to see very well, but I was big, strong and angry.

I lived only a half-hour car ride from New York City, and sometimes I'd accompany my friends into the city for a night of drinking and fun. After a few drinks, I'd play my own game of "chicken." As my friends and I walked down the sidewalk, I'd walk on ahead of them and then dart into the middle of a busy Manhattan street, daring taxicabs to run me over. Instead, the cabbies would screech their brakes, honk their horns, and swerve in the nick of time to miss me.

I didn't realize how screwed up I was mentally. I was suffering, in agony really, and suicidal tendencies were showing themselves. All of my anger provided a platform for a very dangerous and unhealthy situation. I was beginning to make my family and friends uncomfortable. I was like a Jekyll and Hyde, lashing out in frustration. But I couldn't seem to help myself.

Everyone around me knew I was losing my eyesight. When I went out at night with my friends, I had to grab an arm and be steered around. I felt like a burden to them. They were always picking me up and driving me around. I didn't realize that they did these things for me willingly, because they genuinely cared for me. Instead I just felt like I was an albatross to them.

My morals were also at a low ebb. My self-pity over going blind somehow let me justify fooling around with as many girls as I could. They didn't mean much to me. I didn't love myself so I certainly couldn't love someone else. My lack of a real relationship with a woman was a manifestation of my low self-esteem and distress over what was happening to me.

I was angry with life. My faith was shattered. I didn't think it was fair or that I deserved a burden like blindness. Now I know that I was immature in my thinking. I hadn't yet realized my purpose.

It was the fall of 1981 when I seriously began to question whether I was making an impact on my students as their teacher. I thought I'd be doing the Belleville school system and myself a big favor by resigning. I didn't think of my future, that I might wind up selling pencils or apples on a street corner. It was just that my pride was hurting.

My eyesight had become so bad that I had to ask some students to correct tests for me. This didn't sit well with me. I began to feel like I couldn't do my job. I knew there were others at the school who doubted my ability, and now I doubted it, too. Finally, I went to see the principal of Belleville High, Michael Lally.

"Mr. Lally, I have to resign. I can't see the students' faces any longer. Everyone knows it. I can't read their papers. I can't give them grades, and I can't tell if they're cheating or not."

Tears were streaming down my face. I tried to hide them, but I couldn't. It was my moment of truth.

But Mr. Lally surprised me. "Listen to me, Richard. You are not going to quit," he said. "What do you need to continue teaching?"

I could scarcely believe what I was hearing. I had expected the complete opposite. I told him I would need a proctor to monitor tests and a teacher's aide to grade papers.

"I'll make sure you get what you need. I don't want to lose you. I've never heard a negative word about you from parents, students, or anyone in this town. You are highly revered and respected. If you need anything, just come and ask."

I was stunned at his unconditional faith in me. I said, "You'll never regret this. I'm going to work that much harder to prove you made the right decision. I won't let you down."

Walking into the principal's office was the lowest point in my life, but it was also the turning point. I walked out of that office on a cloud. I knew what I must do.

He had given me a new shot of confidence. Somebody believed in me. It had been a long while since I had faced the truth and put what was most important to me on the line: my integrity. I felt exhilarated.

I wouldn't let my handicap stop me. From that point on, I wanted to be the best teacher and role model I could be.

If you had told me then that in 1985, just four years later, I would be selected as Princeton University's Distinguished High School Teacher of the Year, I wouldn't have believed it. Nor would I have guessed that one day I would be selected to represent my profession in both my state and my country.

Yes, I had plummeted to where I felt I was looking up at the bottom of my shoes. But when I faced the truth and looked forward to my life instead of dwelling in negativity, I began to rebound.

And I haven't stopped moving forward yet!

When we hit rock bottom we become so steeped in negativity that we can't believe there's anything positive remaining in our lives. All we think of is the deep valley of despair that we're mired in. And the more we Dwell On Negative Thoughts (D-O-N-T), the more difficult it is to dig out of that hole. And it can happen to anyone.

It's easy to resign ourselves, to feel we can't succeed because the odds are stacked against us. Anyone can fall prey to thinking that way. I'm glad not everybody does.

Thomas Edison provides a good example of refusing to fall into negative thinking. In his attempt to invent the incandescent lamp, he failed hundreds of times. He had every reason to quit, but his failures energized him all the more. Once he was asked, "How did you have the energy and perseverance to continue after so many failures?" Edison quipped in his usual fashion, "I found every way to fail and the only way left was the way to succeed."

If we can adopt Edison's thinking into our own lives, all of a sudden that valley that seemed so deep can transform itself into a ladder with a way out. And each step of the way out, each little success can lead to bigger future successes.

When I plummeted, just as many of you have, I had turned off that little switch of positive thinking within myself. When we decide to turn it back on, we can use all of those gut-wrenching obstacles that we stumbled upon as our stepping stones to success. Like all of those who succeed, champions rise from the dust of their own defeats.

If we recognize that our frightening plummet and negative experiences are the dues we must pay to appreciate success, then we can view them as simply a necessary part of our journey, put there so that we remain humble and appreciative for the wonderful successes that life can present to us.

When we learn to replace negative thought with positive thought we've reached the first step in climbing out of the valley. Positive thought is good, but it must be turned into positive action or it is wasted.

When we intellectualize, we may challenge the negative demons that hold us back in our minds. But when we *actualize* and put our positive plan into action, we bury these demons forever.

Most people, when their "woe is me" factor is at its highest point, won't even attempt to rise out of their valley. They start to curse and use the four-letter word that Doubting Thomases always utter: "C-A-N-T!" Champions turn that around, not only on the fields of competition, but in the great game of life. For champions, C-A-N-T means something different. They drop the letter "T," and now they C-A-N. They have Courage and Confidence, they take Action and Never stop until they reach their personal victories in life.

Sometimes we don't know how good we have it until we lose something. Those are the "dues" I referred to earlier. If life were easy and everyone always succeeded, it would not only be boring, we'd never discover the mentors and leaders we all need.

Inside the word "plummet" is a "plum." And sometimes, even in the midst of our worst personal tragedies, there might be a plum waiting to be discovered. This fruit leaves a sweet taste in our mouths when we realize that from negative experiences we can create positive pathways to our future.

Not everyone needs to plummet. Some people can by-pass this step. If your life is going well, don't leap into a valley on purpose. If your life's fortunes enable you to steer around pitfalls, indeed if this chapter may help you avoid pitfalls, then you will have more time and energy to spend on the six P's in the following chapters that will positively enhance performance and give you the P-E-P you will need to succeed in your life's mission.

CHAPTER TWO
"PRIDE"

"Whenever I do anything in life, I think of my ancestors. I possess the genes and heredity of every one of my predecessors in every cell of my body. I carry them with me with pride and dignity."

To many people the word "pride" conjures up thoughts of braggadocio, an attitude that leads someone to believe he or she is better than the next person.

That is not the kind of pride I am talking about. As partners on planet Earth, each and every person should take pride in who we are and where we came from, pride in the beauty and power of nature and in protecting our environment, and very importantly, pride in our ancestors, our parents and grandparents.

These are the people who have gone before us and are smiling down upon us in the hope that we are carrying on their ancestral pride with dignity and respect.

As a high school biology teacher, I am enthralled with the mystery of life and I attempt to convey this awe to my students. One of the most incredible mysteries I talk about is how each student's chromosomes carry all the traits of every one of their ancestors who came before, going all the back to the dawn of mankind.

Because every human being shares the same ancestral tree, it's natural that we all feel pride in the things we do. When we think about how our ancestors are part of us, we can go forth not in a selfish manner, but in a way that reflects positively on our forebears.

I have received much of my personal pride from my family foundations. My parents are a very big part of my life. I take pride in what they have accomplished, that despite difficult circumstances, they still raised five children successfully.

This is what our country needs in the worst way: an infusion of family values and a getting back to family first.

While I may have won many gold medals for the United States of America, the true gold, I believe wholeheartedly, is in one's family.

I have been greatly influenced by members of both my immediate and extended family. It was family pride that helped me rise from my devastating plummet.

"There are two kinds of people in this world. Those who DON'T and those who DO. Those who DON'T Dwell On Negative Thoughts. They think but don't act. They never get anywhere. Those who DO may be Driven and Obsessive, or Determined and Obstinate, or Dutiful and Obedient, the latter being the true humble champions in life. These are the people who reach their goals, because they DO."

I was a skinny little kid from a second generation Italian-American working-class family. My dad, Joe Ruffalo, started working at age eight, and didn't stop working for the next 68 years. His father, Antonio, died when Dad was six years old and his mother, Saveria, died under suspicious circumstances while collecting rent monies. My father was only 12.

For years my dad worked seven days a week at two or three different jobs to support his growing family. We called him "Plop," a variation of "Pop" that seemed to fit because he'd come home from work so tired, he'd simply plop down in his chair. Although he was never at home as much as we children would have liked, when he was he always had time for each one of us. We all looked forward to taking turns sitting on his lap and having him tell us poems and stories. To this day, he is one of the funniest, wittiest storytellers I've ever heard. That was one of his ways of bestowing his love upon his children.

My mother, Rose, is the same age as my father. She grew up in the tough Red Hook section of Brooklyn, New York, one of 14 children in a very strict, regimented, patriarchal Sicilian family. Their lives were steeped in tradition, everybody kissing hello and good-bye and showing respect at mealtime by sitting in the proper seat from the oldest on down to the youngest.

Mom's father, Frank Sconzo, was something else, a Runyonesque character if there ever was one. Grandpa Sconzo was a throwback, an adventurer who sought a better life. In the early part of this century, he left his family in Italy and set out for America. Fresh off the boat and knowing no English, he settled down in Brooklyn where he eventually married and raised a large family of children that included four doctors.

He certainly was not a handsome man, looking something like a cross between Groucho Marx and Alfred Hitchcock. In his calf-length socks and garters below his long walking shorts, speaking with his thick broken-English accent, he made quite an impression on people.

But his looks were deceiving. Although he didn't receive much formal education, my grandfather was as sharp as any man alive. He was resourceful and knew how to take advantage of an opportunity, like the time he was a bootlegger during the Prohibition. He was the patriarch of the family who took care of everyone, and his advice on a variety of topics was eagerly sought by all. He had many wonderful memories of his life, and we grandkids loved to sit at his knee and have him tell us stories.

I have a great fondness for my grandfather. I like to think that a large part of my personality was inspired by him.

Sometimes Grandpa would pile the five Ruffalo kids into his car and take us down to the beach at Sandy Hook. As we pulled into the parking lot, he went into his routine. He'd tell the attendant how he had a bad heart and couldn't walk too far, so could he please park in that reserved spot right next to the prime beach.

The fellow couldn't help but grant the poor old guy with five kids his wish, so we'd always end up with the best parking spot. Once out of the car, my grandfather would walk very slowly and painfully until he was out of the attendant's line of sight—then sprint onto the beach and dive head first into the ocean.

As kids, all we could do was watch with our jaws agape and wonder how time and again Grandpa could pull this off. I think he did it just to see the looks on our faces.

Later, he'd take us to the food stand on the beach and fiddle around with the clams. Although he knew the clams were two dollars a dozen, he'd take them to the cash register and just pull one dollar out of his pocket. The man behind the counter would say, "Hey Pops, it's two bucks." Grandpa would look in the other pocket and pull out nothing but lint. Then he'd grab my hand and, with a pitiful look on his face, say in his broken English, "Come on, Richie, let's go. We no can buy it. Put everytin' back."

It never failed. The guy at the counter would invariably feel sorry for him and say, "Hey, Pops, it's okay. Take whatever you want."

He'd load up the bag with enough for all of us, and walk outside real slow until he got out of the line of sight. Then he'd sprint to the car and hand us the food with smile on his face and a twinkle in his eyes. He knew how to make us feel special.

Grandpa knew how to put one over on us, too. I remember one Sunday when I was about 12, we had a backyard family picnic at our house. My older brother Joe and I had the bright idea of having a basketball shooting contest.

My father had set up a basketball hoop and backboard for my older brother Joe and me in our backyard. Day after day, we practiced on it; we got to be pretty good shooters, too. For our basketball contest, we put a dollar in a pot and invited each of our uncles to do the same. Whoever made the most baskets out of 10 foul shots would win the pot. Back in the early 1960s, 12 dollars was a lot of money to us kids. It could buy a heckuva a lot of baseball cards, candy, sodas and toys.

My brother and I made a pact that if either of us came out first in the contest, we'd split the $12 pot. Naturally, we felt we had the home court advantage, having practiced constantly on that basket. We fully expected to beat our uncles out of their money, especially since they weren't as athletically inclined as we were.

My brother took the lead when he made six of his 10 shots, and I did even better, sinking eight. Just as I prepared to grab the pot, my grandfather, now about 70 years old, came over, asking what was going on.

We explained to him about the contest, so he decided to put his dollar into the pot and give it a try. When he walked up to the foul line, we had to bite our lips to keep from laughing. Here was this little old bow-legged, chubby guy from the old country, standing at the foul line with the ball between his legs, about to shoot underhanded like Wilt Chamberlain.

Well, Grandpa Sconzo knew how to shut us up. He proceeded to swish nine out of his 10 shots to win the pot. We were silenced, our jaws dropping to our knees. Grandpa had done it to us again.

Each year in my home town of Bloomfield, the Town Olympics were held for all the school kids to prove themselves in track. I was the fastest youngster at Brookside Elementary School, and in the fourth, fifth and sixth grades I represented my class in the 50-yard dash in these town-wide races.

The contestants vied for trophies awarded to the top three finishers in each race. To win one of those trophies was what I wanted more than anything in the world. In fourth and fifth grades, I failed to win one, but by sixth grade, I felt my time had come. I was a little faster, a little stronger, and I had my sights set on a trophy.

In my eyes, having a trophy would make me a star, like Mickey Mantle, the star of the New York Yankees, who was my boyhood hero. If I had a trophy, I could impress all the kids from the other schools, including the girls whom I'd begun to notice, and maybe even my teachers.

I easily won my heat in the trials. By the time the

runners were called for the finals, my adrenaline was really pumping and I was ready to fly.

Paul Williams, the coach from the Bloomfield High School team who would be my coach there four years later, was the starter. "On your mark, get set ..... go!" He waited so long to say "Go!" I was thrown off stride and got out of the blocks dead last.

The race was on. I made up a lot of ground and was really moving through the crowd. When I looked up, I saw the first and second place runners and no one else. I was on the far outside lane and I appeared to be two strides ahead of everyone else. If I could hold onto third place, I'd get my long-awaited trophy.

When we arrived at the tape, the winner was George Drew, who by his senior year at Bloomfield High would be one of the best quarter-milers in New Jersey and earn a scholarship to Michigan State. The runner-up was a skinny kid named Nicky Zungoli who would team with Drew as part of a record-breaking mile relay team for Bloomfield in 1969 and earn himself a scholarship to Clemson University.

And then there was Rich Ruffalo in third place, in rather select company. I was ecstatic. I had finally achieved my trophy. Or so I thought. Unfortunately, the place pickers and timers had missed me. They picked a kid who finished on the inside lane, closer to them.

I knew I had beaten him by three strides, and for the moment I was crushed. But my friends and classmates knew I should have won the trophy, and I knew it in my heart.

I was hurt for a while, but even so, I was proud of my effort. I put it down as a simple mistake on the part of the judges and just took pride in knowing I was one of the best runners for my age in the whole town of Bloomfield.

I could laugh about that disappointment a couple of years later when Drew and Zungoli became my teammates on the high school track team. By then I was a tall and lanky javelin thrower who took pride in winning a varsity letter and helping Bloomfield win the state track and field championship our senior year. It was the first and only time it happened!

Years later, early in my career as a member of the United States Association for Blind Athletes, I had to learn about pride all over again.

After battling my blindness for 10 years, and finally accepting it in the early 1980s, I rededicated my purpose in life with athletics playing an important part.

During the winter of 1984-85, I was pumping iron three or four times a week in preparation for power lifting competition and to become stronger for my other events in the javelin, shot put and discus. I wanted to win every event in which I was competing on a world-class level.

I wanted to be a blind athlete people would remember: a well-rounded, diversified athlete and a champion in many sports arenas. I wanted to have my name on the record books so people could refer to me and think of me in a positive manner.

My message through sports would transcend winning and losing. That message would be that anyone can overcome any obstacle. I felt that was my mission. Now I had a reason for existence.

I realized this was my burden, my own cross to bear. I remembered a tale that was once told to me about a man who complained that he was going blind. He was taken to a room full of crosses.

"These are the crosses that everyone on earth bears, that everyone must carry sometime in life," he was told.

Some crosses were huge. Some were the size of two telephone poles.

The blind man was told, "I'll let you trade your cross of blindness for any cross in this place."

The man, who had been granted temporary sight, looked around the place and saw each cross had a person's name tag on it, but he couldn't make out the names. He picked out the smallest cross he could find, one the size of two match sticks. "I'll take the one over there, behind the redwood tree crosses," he said.

"You can't pick that one."

"Why not?" the man asked.

"Because your name is already on that cross. It's your own cross of blindness, the cross you were meant to bear."

That put the man's impending blindness into proper perspective. Everything is relative. Everyone thinks his or her situation is the worst of all, until he or she sees the next person's problem. That's just human pride.

For me, blindness is only as bad as I want it to be. The story of the man who had no shoes and complained until he met the man who had no feet illustrates the same point.

Although I had lost my eyesight, I decided to continue on my quest to be the best I could be by becoming a positive role model for the rest of my life. That's what I would truly take pride in.

I would be a positive force and never give up. I would make the most out of my life, enjoy it to the fullest, and try to help other people.

By the mid-1980s, my athletic career really took off. When I returned to teach at Belleville High in fall of 1985, people treated me in an entirely different light. Even my students showed more interest.

They were all looking at me as a role model. I had accomplished my mission. I was helping kids and I was loving it.

Anyone who has ever reached the top of their profession can't deny that ego is involved in the rise to the top. After we accept this, we must remember that to be a true champion, we must also possess other important qualities.

A "C-H-A-M-P" has Confidence, is Hard-working, develops Altruism, acts as a Mentor and Perseveres.

Let's expand upon each of these.

CONFIDENCE:

Confidence is not cockiness. Cocky people try to pass themselves off as something other than what they are. They live empty lives, putting on their best Oscar-winning performance to try and remain constantly in character that isn't real. Their insecurities drive them to develop a superiority complex, which actually masks their true feelings of inferiority.

This behavior breeds a negative aura that envelopes that individual; and though he or she may seem to emit a sense of pride, it is negative, destructive, false emotion. This is not real pride, but simple narcissism that erodes our society. It does nothing to nourish the soul of the person or the community.

Confidence is the antithesis of cockiness. Confident people give off a positive aura and a strong belief in them-selves. They see the big picture and understand that their mission is larger than their own personal desires.

Confident individuals are champions and winners in life. They are not afraid of challenges. They adapt to change and know they will settle for nothing less than their best. They are important role models for our society.

Confidence breeds more confidence. The more self-confident a person feels, the easier it is to find those positive pathways to good fortune and success.

Confident people believe that obstacles are not bar-riers, but rather hurdles to be leapt over as they continue toward the finish line. Their commitment to positive goal-setting, achievement and continual reassessment allows them to be victorious in their race. For confident people, finish lines often become starting lines for the next mission.

Confidence is not arrogance. It means feeling good just knowing that others may find inspiration, strength and direction from what you have accomplished.

HARD WORK:

Hard-working people prove that it's not how you start in life, but how you finish. Our nation was built on the backs of all of the diverse immigrants who came to this country and added the best elements of their culture to America's quilt of humanity. Woven together, the strands of excellence and hard work from around the world, brought by our nation's forefathers and immigrants, has completed a masterpiece quilt.

Most of the immigrants who built America came from humble beginnings and showed their families that hard work truly pays off. The result? Today's United States, the world's most powerful economic and social leader.

We must eliminate the influence of negative people who think they're entitled to the fruits of everyone else's labor. Such an attitude rips out the strands of the quilt of hard work. Instead, let's teach them how to add to our quilt and make it expand.

The best way to teach is by example. We need only to look at the hard workers in our families and our communities to find our positive role models. Let's give them the respect and glory they deserve and follow their example.

ALTRUISM:

The old saying "It is better to give than to receive" has endured because it has been proven to be true in many different ways.

Giving from the heart brings so much back to you. When you give, relish the feelings of charity and selflessness that come from enriching and strengthening through your efforts. Humanitarianism, good-Samaritanism and empathy add dimension to your life. The glow on the face of a giving person, indeed their soul or their aura or whatever you might call it, is magnified through their magnanimity and charitable acts of kindness toward others.

Finding a cause to support that is greater than our own desires and helps us to achieve greater glories. It adds great meaning to our life's mission when we know countless others may benefit positively from our deeds.

MENTORS:

When you think you have all the answers, when you think you know it all, it's time to leave this earth. The more we know and the more we more learn, the more we realize how much there is to learn and how little we really know. Every time a discovery is made, individually or globally, it kicks up a stone in the road and underneath that stone lies new turf, a new domain yet to be traveled upon.

Successful people understand there's never one answer to a question. They appreciate another point of view and they seek advice and guidance from many sources. Take this book, for example. It is just one source of information and inspiration to help our pursuit of excellence.

What is most important is that we all reach out, listen, and learn from as many different sources and people as possible to create our own broader and deeper understanding of life. We all need mentors—those people who guide us through the tough times, who have been there before, who can take us around detours and help speed up our journey toward success. Why waste time and energy? Mentors help us maximize our potential by reaching our goals more quickly, thereby leaving even more time to reach new and loftier goals.

An open mind and a healthy humility about one's limitations is critical to the successful person. And to accept a mentor's advice is to do a good deed as well. Mentors enjoy giving guidance to others who may benefit from their wisdom, appreciate having the opportunity to give back something for the success they have found.

This is the essence of the dedicated teacher who shows students how to reach new heights, both in the classroom and in their lives. There is no way to quantify the value of such an endeavor; the reward for both teacher and student is priceless.

A CHAMP is not in it for the income, but for the outcome.

PERSEVERANCE:

Having perseverance reminds me of being like a mighty oak tree. If that oak has strong roots firmly planted in the ground, it doesn't matter how big it is or how many branches it has, when the coldest winter comes, the roots have stored enough nourishment to help that tree survive.

When we persevere, we strengthen our roots. Every time we surface from a tough situation and are victorious, we must remember that experience. The next time adversity strikes, we know we can prevail. The easiest thing to do when times are tough is to quit. But, as the saying goes, "Winners never quit and quitters never win."

We need to remember that although the road to success may be paved with failures, it is always under construction.

The five qualities that comprise "C-H-A-M-P" will help us become top achievers in school, athletics, career and life. They can help instill that positive pride we need, the kind that leaves a positive effect not just on ourselves, but on everyone who comes in contact with us during our lifetime.

CHAPTER THREE
"PRESSURE"

"In life there are no overachievers,
only underestimators."

Everyone feels pressure. Champions rise to the occasion when placed under pressure, because pressure enhances performance for champions. So many people feel that they can't handle pressure; they just give up assuming they can't rise to the challenge. But I can offer some insight on how to do just that.

When I went to see my principal that fateful day in 1981 to tender my resignation, it put me on the road to handling pressure. He taught me a valuable lesson that day: Don't underestimate yourself. Because he believed in me, I started to believe in myself. And with that belief came a renewed determination to give my best, to succeed at what I loved doing the most.

When you think you can't handle the pressure, when you feel like you want to quit, don't. Believe in yourself. There is no need to feel ashamed if you try and fail, only of you fail to try.

"Life is a test. There are those who choose to prepare for the test and pass, and others who choose to complain and make excuses. Champions don't make excuses when they fail, they make plans to succeed in the future."

In 1986, I was a member of the United States Association for Blind Athletes team as a competitor in the javelin in the World Championships for the Disabled in Goteborg, Sweden.

Although I had already set a world record with a throw of 45.26 meters, I wanted to prove myself on the field against the best in the world, the competitors who had come to Sweden. Even the Russians, who had boycotted the 1984 Paralympics, were in attendance. They had a reputation for sending only those athletes who had a chance at winning the gold medal.

I knew their javelin thrower had accumulated some impressive statistics. He had thrown at the 42-meter mark previously and was certainly capable of defeating me.

The officials at this meet were very strict with the athletes. Coaches were forbidden to say anything at all to their athletes. This made it especially difficult for the blind athletes to achieve their best marks.

At the time, I had a short, cropped beard that I had sported for the past 12 years. I had grown it in 1974 to make me look tougher and older than my students. I had promised my sponsors, who were less than thrilled with this image, that if I won a gold medal I would return home clean-shaven.

The Russian threw first, and sure enough, he got off a good throw, measured at 41 meters. I then uncorked my first throw, looking for a mark, and I came in at 40 meters. The Norwegian thrower landed in third place at 38.6 meters. I sensed the competition would come down to a duel between myself and my Russian counterpart.

On his next throw, the Russian added more distance getting it out to 42 meters, while my second throw did not improve my distance. The Russian winged a beauty on his third try, setting the pace at 43.66 meters, which really put the pressure on me. My third throw was no better than the first, and I began to worry. Adding to my dwindling confidence was the pain I was feeling from a tender groin muscle I had pulled in practice three weeks earlier.

It would all come down to my fourth and final attempt. I had to beat the Russian's mark of 43.66. Nagging little doubts crept into to my mind. How could I win this competition against such a strong opponent when I wasn't in top physical form?

And then I stopped and thought about what I was doing. I was giving myself an excuse to fail. I had regressed into my old self-indulgent ways, getting ready to quit and blame it on something other than myself. I felt ashamed.

I felt a new determination to win, but I knew I needed help. I looked up and asked for the strength to heave my mightiest throw.

I ran down the runway and let out a warrior's yell. I knew my body was in the correct position. I felt a little extra boost in my right arm that I could not explain. The throw was measured at 47.08 meters.

Not only had I beaten the Russian, but I had broken the official world record!

I felt great. I had tears in my eyes. I had finally captured my long-sought world javelin title on the field. Of course, it also meant the end of my beloved beard. Oh well, a small price to pay for such a tremendous thrill.

That day I had a revelation. With hard work, determination to succeed, and faith, anyone can conquer worlds and move mountains.

I know, because it happened to me.

It wasn't until the next year, when I competed in the Canadian-American Games in Long Island on July 28, 1987, that I would face such intense pressure again. I was scheduled to compete in the 220-pound weight class in power lifting, as well as the javelin, shot put and discus field events.

I was concentrating on the weight lifting at this event because, if I did well, I could win a spot on the United States team that would compete in the World Championships in April, 1988. That was the ultimate goal for which I was training.

I had lost weight, trimming down to 218 pounds to qualify for the 220-pound weight class. However, losing weight meant losing strength so I had trained especially hard to maintain that physical power.

I opened with the squat event and came through it okay. I moved on to the next event, the bench press, almost immediately. Because there so many competitors, the contest had the atmosphere of a three-ring circus, a marathon of endurance as we went from event to event.

In the bench press, I had planned to open with 308 pounds. But I felt weak. I had thrown the discus earlier that day and hadn't eaten much, still worrying about making weight for my weight class.

As I went to the bench press, I knew a lot of people were watching me. I wanted desperately to do well and earn a spot on the United States World Team. I was feeling the pressure.

The officials handed me the bar with the weight at 308 pounds. I attempted the lift, but couldn't raise the bar. The position of the bar was too low on my chest, too close to my belly, making it difficult to lock out my elbow.

The spotters saw my distress. They grabbed the weight from me and put it back on the rack. I had wasted my first lift; only two remained. I thought back to the time I bombed out of a competition in 1983. I hadn't failed since and I didn't want to fail here.

I took a short break and went for the 308 pounds a second time. The spotters handed me the bar and asked me three times if I was sure had it. Each time I answered affirmatively.

I took the weight and immediately proceeded to drop it from three feet over my head, right down onto my chest and sternum. All the air inside me escaped in one swift whoosh. I felt like my eyes popped out of my head.

The crowd that had been lulled to sleep by boredom suddenly came to life. Their nervous chatter filled the air and I heard frightened voices near me calling for trainers and medical assistance.

I was still lying on the bench, wheezing and short of breath. Finally, they pulled the weights off me. I had cracked my sternum and upper ribs. I was more than physically hurt; I was embarrassed and upset.

Somehow, I had let my wrists lock out, so that they came forward and let the bar fall out of my hands. "What could be worse?" I thought to myself. "Now, I've seriously hurt myself. I don't have a chance of being a world champion now."

I was afraid I might have punctured a lung, which can lead to severe internal bleeding and even death. I sat up and tried to breathe; it was painful and difficult. As I walked off the platform, trainers came over to guide me, sit me down and apply ice to my chest.

After several minutes, I began to breathe a little better. My chest ached terribly. When I turned to the right side, my rib cage seemed to open up like a gate, bringing with it intense pain.

My coach, John Schrock, wanted to take me to the hospital for x-rays. I heard the voice on the loudspeaker say: "Ruffalo, three minutes to attempt. Final attempt."

I asked my coach to put his hands up. As I pushed my palms against his in a bench-press position, he asked me what I was doing.

"Coach, it doesn't hurt any more when I press than when I'm not pressing," I told him. "Let me give it a try."

The loudspeaker blared again: "Ruffalo, one minute."

I strode to the platform. I laid down on the bench and asked for the weights. I brought the bar down on my chest and the official clapped his hands, signaling me to start pushing upwards.

I pressed it up, letting out a groan, but getting it up with no problem at all. The bar went up as straight as an arrow. The lift counted. I had bench pressed 308 pounds.

The gymnasium erupted in spontaneous applause and cheering. I had heard all the Doubting Thomases in the room. I had felt them all around me. But I knew I had been given the strength to triumph over the pressure. It was the easiest lift I had made in a long time. Even though my chest was aching, I had executed simply and correctly and the pain momentarily disappeared.

I felt that little extra help again. My weight lift total, combined with my total in the squat and dead lift categories, carried me to a gold medal in my weight class.

I had overcome the pressure to earn that coveted spot on the U.S. World Team. In fact, the pressure gave me the extra P.E.P. to enhance my performance that day.

Two years later, in the spring of 1989, I married my girlfriend, Dianne. Our wedding day was wonderful. It was so full of our love for each other and our honeymoon was as romantic as we could have ever wished for. A few weeks later, my wife gave me the best news of my life: we were going to have a baby. Imagine me a daddy! We were thrilled.

The next few months went beautifully for us. We were happily looking forward to the arrival of our baby and Dianne was doing well with the pregnancy. Then, one day her foot slipped and she felt a sharp pain in her back. She had herniated a disc. Dianne was in so much pain the doctor told her to take it easy and stay off her feet. This meant she had to stop working, to give up a job she had loved so much. It also meant that, without Dianne's paycheck coming in each week, times would be tough. I knew I would have to provide better for my new family. I racked my brain to find ways to enhance my income. I felt tremendous anxiety about our situation and an intense pressure to support my family. As an athlete, I had appreciated the support of many sponsors whose help had made it possible for me to participate in athletic events throughout the world. I figured I might be able to pay them back by delivering speeches to various groups with which they were affiliated. My speeches were so well received that I started getting calls from other groups that would pay for my presentations. I began networking as much as I could, spending hours on the telephone trying to line up speaking engagements.

My new career started off slowly, but I was patient and determined. My first opportunities to speak were to church groups, school groups, and groups of disabled people. I shared my message with these audiences: how the human spirit could rise over any difficult circumstance. I found people to be very receptive. They believed me because I was living proof of the power of that message.

In retrospect, my whole life seemed to be a struggle until I rose to the challenge that pressure offers, meaning accepting responsibility and learning to put things in the proper perspective. Pressure became much easier to handle once I began doing things for others rather than myself.

Slowly, steadily, my speaking engagements began to increase and I was able to contribute more to my family's financial stability. Again, I was thankful for having been given the ability and the courage to get up and speak in front of a room full of people without a single note, to communicate my messages in coherent, memorable reference points, and to truly feel appreciated by my audiences.

Champions in any endeavor come to understand, even anticipate, pressure because they know they won't be successful until they meet their challenge and overcome it.

Champions are their own worst critics and best allies. They seem to have an inner voice that tells them how to handle pressure and rise above it.

In my life, pressure presents itself in four different but important ways.

The first is spiritual pressure. That is, knowing what kind of pressure others have endured and realizing that our own tribulations are insignificant when compared to those of others who have gone before us.

The second is family pressure in that a provider must do whatever it takes to fulfill his or her family's needs. He or she wants to take the pressure and stress out of their lives by providing for them in the best way possible.

The third is career pressure. We all have jobs to do, and it is important that we do them as best we can, not only to provide for our families, but to reach new heights, even discover new talents.

That's what happened for me when I became a motivational speaker. The pressure I felt made me push myself until I found a way to utilize my talents and solve my problem. As I said at the beginning of this chapter, my ability to face pressure began when I promised my principal I would repay his faith in me. The pressure I put on myself not to let anyone down has made me a better teacher, a better speaker, a better person.

Every day when I enter the classroom or step up on the podium to deliver a speech, people realize my eyes are permanently closed. They see a person who has succeeded under pressure and in spite of a disability; they realize they can do the same in their lives. I put this across every day to my students whose lives I touch and to whom I have a tremendous responsibility. I hope that they benefit from my philosophy and carry it with them when they go out into the world so that they can help themselves and others.

The fourth is athletic pressure. Compared to the other pressures, this may be the least important. But I see sports as a microcosm of life. Athletes battle pressure, encounter physical and mental challenges, and must work hard to achieve their goal. I think people of all walks of life can empathize with their struggles and appreciate their victories.

Each year a phenomenon takes place which I call "Olympic highs." People will watch a major athletic event unfold, become inspired and head to the gym to begin a new physical regimen. Those who stick with their new physical awareness become better human beings because they feel good physically and mentally. They set little goals for themselves in the gym and learn to do the same in their careers and with their families. They build confidence and self-esteem by doing something good for their bodies which, in turn, becomes something good for the soul.

Everyone feels pressure. Replacing the negative pressures with positive ones is an important lesson we must all learn. Those people who can do so are traveling down the road to success; and even if they get sidetracked, they have started along the path of overcoming pressure and are moving in the right direction.

That's what makes champions.

CHAPTER FOUR
"PURPOSE"

*"My aspiration is to be an inspiration
from now until forever."*

Having purpose means dealing with things greater than one's self. Sometimes life deals us lemons, but instead of turning sour, why not make lemonade?

I have dealt with my cross of blindness by tapping my human potential to overcome my condition. As a teacher, I hope to teach my students that by adapting to dramatic changes in life, one can still be a success and typify excellence.

Sharing my experiences with others allows me to demonstrate that they, too, have hidden talents to discover, and it's only a matter of time until they find their purpose and become a success in life.

"The human potential is like buried treasure. It rises to the surface with courage and can be salvaged by faith."

It took me a while to find my purpose, but once I did, I learned that life is exciting, significant and worth living, and I share that point of view with anyone who will listen. I believe in the Greek philosophy of sound mind and sound body. By enhancing their health, people improve the quality of their lives and lengthen their life span. This gives them more time to share with those they love, preserving a legacy of good will for their family and for all those whose lives they touch. To me, this is truly the essence of life.

"Even if you're less than enthusiastic about something you're doing, keep a smile on your face. You may even come to enjoy it and be able to share your newfound energy with others."

During my grade school days, I had to walk one mile from my parents' house to Brookside School. At about the halfway point, I had to cross the very busy intersection of Broad and Pitt Streets. On this corner stood a crossing guard known only to the children as "Jim."

Jim was probably in his forties, painfully thin, with wire-rimmed glasses on his long, gaunt face. I thought he looked like a human skeleton. He constantly shook like a leaf and never spoke. He was a very odd person.

Nonetheless, in every kind of weather—snow, sleet, rain—this fellow would guide school kids across the street. He'd take my hand and, even though he wouldn't talk, he'd communicate that he took seriously his responsibility to deliver us safely to the other side of the street. I thought of Jim as a kindly Good Samaritan. Many of the kids thought he was retarded and, of course, made fun of him. But others like myself felt quite the opposite and often stuck up for him.

During inclement weather, Jim would wear an old raincoat or frayed parka. It was evident even to us kids that Jim didn't have much money. Still, he'd often reach into his pocket and with a trembling hand give us a stick of gum or a piece of candy. Although he had nothing, he was willing to share what little he had with others.

A policeman patrolled the corner where Jim crossed us and one day I asked the policeman about Jim. I wanted to know why Jim had a number tattooed on his wrist. The policeman couldn't tell me. Perhaps, he didn't want to.

It wasn't until much later that I learned the truth about Jim. The number on his wrist was branded on him by the Nazis when he was interned in a concentration camp during

World War II. They also cut out his tongue so he could never speak again. His constant shaking was no doubt the result of the severe trauma he had suffered. Jim was a survivor of the Holocaust, a courageous person whom every kid should have looked up to.

I admired Jim for having a purpose. He inspired me simply by the fact he was there to help people, particularly children whom he loved, despite the absolute horror that he had lived through.

I have wished many times that I had an opportunity to sit and talk with him and discover what insights he might share. I feel he's in heaven, and when I make it there, maybe one day I will have that opportunity.

As I grew older and faced more responsibility, I knew that the quality of my life depended on my ability to overcome my handicap.

Although my eyesight was far from perfect when I was young, I loved to read. In the summer, I'd devour four or five books a week. I read on my own because I enjoyed it, because my mind's eye was always better than the television set. I could place the mental pictures anywhere I wanted and it was the best way to learn.

I was always academically minded and competitive. My biggest opponent in the classroom was myself. I had a purpose every school year: to surpass my achievements from the previous year. I didn't just complete an assignment, I gave it my best. I wouldn't settle for being a mediocre student, I wanted to be excellent.

That same purpose has carried over into everything I've done. That's one reason why it was so hard to accept my impending blindness, because I felt it meant that I could no longer excel.

Oddly enough, in another way it helped me, because it made me even more determined to continue to go to school as the curtain of light was falling on me. I wanted to absorb as much education as fast as I could. By the time I was 25, I had earned a master's degree in biology, and later, received a principal/supervisor's certification.

"There are many excuses in life. But there is no excuse for success."

As competitive as I was in the classroom as a student, and now as an educator, I am even more so as an athlete. It's not surprising that it was during an athletic event that I finally uncovered my true purpose in life.

At my first national blind track meet in 1984 in St. Louis, I was ready to rediscover my athletic prowess which had lain dormant since my graduation from college back in 1973. During my collegiate career I was the conference javelin champion and co-captain of the track-and-field team at Montclair State University.

After college, I found that my worsening eyesight made it difficult if not impossible to compete in regular events. It was almost ten years later that I learned of the United States Association for Blind Athletes and the athletic competitions they sponsored. Within a year, I was ready to strut my stuff and reclaim my macho image.

Unfortunately, things didn't work out quite the way I planned.

My first meet was in St. Louis during a heat wave that was oppressive and humid. Because of the difficult conditions, the events at the meet were running late, and javelin throwers were cut to three throws instead of the usual six. My heart sank a bit because if a good mark isn't achieved on the first throw the pressure really begins to build.

My coach went out onto the field and clapped his hands to direct my aim to the center of the field. I ran down the runway, my heart pounding. I got off what I thought was a great throw. It soared out of bounds to the right by 50 feet.

What I had dreaded the most had happened. All javelin throwers hate to lose their first mark. It takes the wind out of your sails. A thrower just wants to get that first mark out of the way to take the pressure off, instead of putting the pressure on with a miss. All I had needed was a halfway decent mark, and then I could have concentrated on getting off a long one on my second and third attempts.

That was my game plan, and I had blown it. My confidence began to ebb away.

I could feel the pressure mounting inside of me. Not only did I want to succeed for myself, I felt I had something to prove. I had already been named to the U.S.A.B.A. international team based on my throws in a meet back home in New Jersey. Many of the officials were getting their first look at me and I hadn't made the impression I wanted with my disqualified first throw.

When my name was called for my second throw, I felt the butterflies flutter in the pit of my stomach, my confidence waning. I remembered back to my college days where my worst meets were always the ones in which I had fouled on my first throw.

Nervously I reviewed my technique. Should I take longer strides or shorter? Should I hold back or throw caution to the wind and give it all I had?

I was thinking too much. That first throw had cast a huge shadow of doubt over my whole being. As I walked reluctantly to my starting mark for my second throw, subconsciously I wanted to walk backward. But something deep inside made me move forward.

I began to tremble. I felt a nervous twinge in my cheek. I was soaked to the quick. The muscles on my back began to twitch.

The signal came. Now, it was all up to me. I blocked out all sound, focusing all my energy forward. I began to jog and then picked up speed, sprinting down the runway with the javelin held high over my shoulder.

I reared back and fired a throw as hard as I could. I let out a fierce guttural sound as I followed through.

The spear went straight up into the air. It probably went over two or three clouds, may even have hit a goose heading south for the winter, and fell to earth just 50 feet away. It was a lollipop throw, and the distance was embarrassing. It landed flat and the official called a foul.

I was left with one final throw. If I thought the pressure was bad before, now it was stifling.

I could sense the energy of the crowd. Many people were there to see me unleash a long throw. They were expecting great things from me. But the Doubting Thomases were there, too, wanting to see me falter and relishing the thought of my impending failure.

I felt like a gladiator in an arena with everyone's thumbs pointing down. My knees were shaking and my legs felt heavy. I could hardly move.

It seemed like from out of nowhere a small group of blind children from a local school for the blind came up to me, led by their teachers. They had been listening to the javelin competition and wanted to come over and "see" me. They did so, feeling my arms and legs, and those little hands touched my heart forever.

As those children touched me, it was as though they had flipped some kind of switch in my body. My engines of anger were at once calmed. I felt both humbled and hopeful and a new feeling of strength spontaneously ignited and surged through my body. My frustration transformed into determination.

These kids had been blind since birth; I had been blessed with sight into my adulthood. I suddenly realized I had taken so many blessings and gifts for granted. I had been able to see smiling faces and beautiful sunsets and brilliant yellow dandelions in a field of lush green grass. I had seen the powerful azure waves of the ocean crashing onto a beach.

These children knew none of this. The touch of their small hands had slain the beast of rage and self-centeredness inside of me and had awakened in me a sleeping giant with a renewed reason for existence.

Suddenly, the picture became crystal clear. I realized why I was there. There were many blind people in this world, many people with other handicaps. They would be watching how I handled adversity and challenge. I realized my destiny was to represent these people, to show that being disabled or handicapped does not mean losing one's courage and determination.

I looked up and asked for the strength to do my best for all of these people. All the people who loved me and believed in me. All the blind people who were there that day, and all the little children who had never even seen the light of day. All the people who think they can't. All the people who lack strength.

My faith was becoming stronger. I believe there is a reason for each of us on this earth. I now knew the reason for my own existence. The light bulb went on inside my head. The picture finally came into focus.

I had let myself fall into the self-pitying thought that I was the only blind person on this earth, the only one suffering this affliction. Of course I wasn't, and finally I realized that I wasn't alone. Hundreds of blind people were competing in this one meet. I now had a chance to be a role model for blind people everywhere. I had found my purpose.

I looked up in the sky and tears started streaming uncontrollably from my eyes. I had never prayed like that in my life. I went back into position for my final throw. I was absolutely focused. I had one thought in mind: to throw and pull this javelin through as hard as I could and to keep my form perfect.

I raced down the runway with tears rolling down my face. I went into a cross-step and planted my foot. I unleashed the javelin and screamed. I couldn't see it, but I heard the crowd cheering and smattering of applause. I

presumed it was a good throw. I stood motionless, await-
ing the official's announcement.

When I heard the measurement, I couldn't believe it.
I had set a world record, breaking the old one by 40 feet!

I achieved that record for all those people to whom I
had dedicated my throw. I had changed my way of thinking,
from performing only for myself to dedicating my efforts to
others, and it had paid off in an unbelievable manner. I now
knew the way I had to live, why I was placed here on earth.
The touch of the little blind children had ignited my purpose.
I now understood and accepted my blindness.

"My eyes have dimmed to open up the eyes of thousands of others."

My eyesight now has been replaced by insight and,
although my visual images are dark, my inner vision for the
future is bright and clear.

As our life path takes its twists and turns, we often
ask why things happen to us. Sometimes, we spend years
searching for answers that only come to us when we have the
faith and courage to stop asking.

My challenge was my blindness. Everyone has their
own trials and tribulations they must endure. It is only when
we find our purpose that we can enhance our performance.
We are able to move from our own individual spheres of influence to a broader scope that affects more than just ourselves.

Although our life's mission may seem difficult, if it
offers inspiration to others, then perhaps it is worthwhile.
When others depend upon us, gaining strength from our

ability to handle adversity, our jets of excellence are refueled and are put into overdrive.

For many of us, our families are more important than ourselves. We are on earth for but a short time, but our legacies live on, embodied in our children and our children's children. This is the focus of our purpose.

> **"I can handle my own disappointment. But I don't want to disappoint others."**

We achieve our purpose when we evolve from thinking as a committee of one to thinking as just one of a committee of many, representing everybody but ourselves.

> **"The three worst reasons for doing something are 'Me, Myself and I.' True achievement comes when you strive to succeed for everyone else but yourself."**

This is our ultimate purpose. Thus purpose can truly enhance performance as evidenced by the stories of many successful people from all walks of life. Throughout history, those people who were truly great and most remembered were those who had a purpose much greater than themselves. They have left a lasting imprint on mankind.

CHAPTER FIVE
"PASSION"

Passion enhances performance.
When people love what they do
they naturally excel.

My father is a perfect example of how passion makes everything worthwhile. He learned to work hard early in life. For most of his adult life, he worked seven days a week, never even taking a vacation, to support his wife and five children. His passion and love for his family is what kept him going. He is a terrific role model and personifies the words "work ethic."

Our heroes are not on television shows or in the movies or in sports arenas. Real heroes are all around us. They're in the living room, sleeping on the couch after a hard day's work supporting their families. They do a great job each and every day, putting everything they have into doing the best they can for their families.

> **"Never stop until the victory you want in life is achieved. If a person truly believes, he can truly achieve. If someone comes up against a wall, he must have the passion to knock it down."**

Some people see a wall and run the other way. Others see the wall and try to stare it down. Walls never blink. Champions climb the wall when it's too tall, dig beneath it when it's too deep, find a way around it when it's too wide. And when none of that succeeds, they chew it down because they know their victories are on the other side.

If a person doesn't believe in what he or she is doing, there is no point in doing it at all.

For me, being a champion in sports feels great, because I've represented my country. But the thrill of victory lasts only as long as the medal ceremony. Once the national anthem is finished, the medal is simply a relic of an event that is now in the past.

Living only for one's self is a shallow existence. Doing things for everyone but one's self is what gives meaning to life. The legacy of good will that comes with helping people is the invisible gold medal that no one can see but us.

While I have been enshrined in several halls of fame, the one hall of fame I desire is heaven, and there is plenty of room there for everyone.

> **"The more invisible gold medals one earns by helping fellow human beings, the lighter they become. The best news of all is that they are the only ones that go with you when you leave this earth."**

I have donated my gold medals to the Italian-American Sports Hall of Fame in Arlington Heights, Illinois, just outside of Chicago, into which I was inducted in 1994. I would much rather have them on public display than collecting dust in a vault somewhere where no one can see them or appreciate what they represent.

Should someone see my display of medals and become inspired because I achieved them with my eyes closed, then that's one more person I've touched and I'm grateful for that.

As a teacher, I believe that I am a role model to students. While I strive to be the best role model I can be to them, I must have a passion for my profession to inspire them to embrace my ideals.

As we approach the 21st century, it is critical that we realize the importance of teachers. They are the gatekeepers to our students' future, to the legacy embodied in our children. They have the significant responsibility of guiding their students over the difficult obstacles that life may present to them on a daily basis.

Teachers must see themselves as role models for excellence and integrity for their students to emulate. Their job, to help young people to adapt to life's changes and find solutions to problems of our society, cannot be overemphasized.

I try to impart a positive collective conscience in each and every student, to teach that together we mold the future, that the decisions we make now will affect our children and our children's children.

Education is the tool that will help us build a better future. Our students' educations must include skills as well as knowledge so that they will be able to find adequate employment, support their families, and nurture the world's most important resource, their children. This is the essence of education, a teacher's timeless gift to our future generations.

I was not always as passionate as I am now about teaching. Back in 1981 I wanted to give up teaching. But my principal's belief in me, his refusal to let me quit something I loved, fueled my passion, and it has grown ever since.

One of my favorite challenges is to get the "cool kids" to think it's cool to do well in school, to understand that good grades aren't just for nerds. I make it clear that the really cool students are the ones who are proud of achieving good grades. Nothing makes me happier than when one of these kids realizes that it is not un-cool to be bright and studious.

Of course, I haven't persuaded everyone. There are a lot of former students pumping gas or working other menial jobs because they thought that looking good in class was more important than studying well.

I have developed my own psychology of teaching which I called educational coaching. This is a natural approach for me since I am an athlete and a coach. In my classes I'm the coach and every student is on my team. I tell my kids that they are part of the "Team of Success," and that they shouldn't look at me as their adversary, but as the manager of their team. My job is to always be there to work with them to help them excel. Their job is to work towards being the best they could be.

That's my philosophy not only in the classroom but on any field of competition.

One of the reasons I decided to try public speaking was that I had developed a passion for my work and I wanted to share with others my enthusiasm and ideas on helping people.

My reason for being had become crystal clear to me. My path would always be straight and true. It felt great to have a real purpose, again thanks to my passion, and to know that after all my pitfalls, I was now a one-hundred-percent positive person.

This was a complete turnaround from just a few years before when I was so negative and depressed that I thought my life was not worth living. At that time I didn't believe in myself; now I believe I can accomplish anything. I am filled with the passion that makes me feel I can do anything I want to do.

Of course, I realize that no one can do everything. We each have to examine ourselves, and learn how to make the most of our strengths and improve on our weaknesses.

During my speeches, I show people how to turn negatives into positives. One my favorite techniques is easy but effective. I ask them to divide a sheet of paper into two columns and write on either side a list of personal negatives and personal positives. I then ask them to put an arrow next to every negative that can be changed so that it points toward the positive column.

"Put that piece of paper in your wallet," I tell my audiences, "and look at it each day. Keep working on the negatives until they turn into positives. Cross out the negatives that cannot be changed and don't waste any more energy on them. The things that can't be changed must simply be accepted. Concentrate only on those negatives that can be changed into positives." People are surprised how well this works. It's simple, anyone can do it, and it's something that stays with them.

Alcoholics Anonymous has a much-repeated saying that supports this exercise: "Grant me the courage to change the things I can, the serenity to accept the things I can't, and the wisdom to know the difference."

There's another saying someone once read to me: "Live for today, dream for tomorrow, and learn from yesterday."

Those are words that inspire us to lead by example, to demonstrate respect for ourselves and others, and to lead lives that will encourage others to follow the road to success and happiness.

These were some of the ideas I touched on when I first started speaking.

Once I was speaking at a school where I met a 15-year-old girl suffering from a terminal illness that was attacking her nervous system. It had gotten so bad that her head had to be held up by a special brace to prevent her windpipe from closing. I was intrigued and touched and wanted to learn more about her.

My speech that day was about heroes. As I weaved my message about true heroes, the audience waited in anticipation for me to reveal my own favorite hero. After mentioning the names of several sports celebrities, any of which could have been a favorite hero in their minds, I paused.

The crowd was completely silent. To their surprise, I spoke the name of the terminally ill girl. I asked someone to push her wheelchair up to where I was standing. I told the crowd that this girl was a true hero whose courage was far greater than the celebrities we so often revere. I praised her for her courage and passion for life, bringing a smile to her face that people described to me as one of great pride, perhaps her first proud smile in a long, long time.

The entire audience stood in uproarious celebration to acknowledge her heroic journey through life. It humbled us all and gave me a wonderful feeling throughout my soul.

Everyone in that audience, including myself, learned a lesson about passion that day. It is a lesson I try to infuse in every speech I deliver.

"He who humbles himself shall be exalted and he who exalts himself shall be humbled."

No matter what we do, passion is the catalyst that can catapult us to higher heights than we've ever imagined. Just passing time on the job, merely getting by day after day isn't really enough to keep the internal hearth flaming. How much more gratifying to embrace our tasks, to look forward to them with youthful enthusiasm despite our age. As my father says, "Age is a matter of mind; if you don't mind, it doesn't matter."

When teaching, I look forward to each and every day because I see that day as a new challenge and a new beginning. Teachers never know when they will touch their students' hearts and help them in their personal metamorphosis, to break out of their cocoon and become a butterfly. The rewards in teaching are wonderful, but difficult to quantify. There's no telling how many caterpillars we as teachers have helped turn into butterflies.

Passion enhances performance for all people in all walks of life. In sports, when there's a reason to win other than just for personal glory, an athlete can reach a zone he or she never knew was possible. If we are passionate people, being positive and see good in all things, good things will happen.

A quote from Adlai Stevenson, back in 1924, says it so well: "I would rather light one candle than curse the darkness." Those words never fail to inspire me.

There's an old cliche about how an optimist and pessimist view a glass of water. The pessimist sees the glass as half-empty. The optimist sees it as half-full. I like to take that idea one step further: The champion sees the glass as overflowing, as the proverbial cup that runneth over, having more water than he needs to succeed.

My passion to do my best and inspire others to do the same has helped light my inner hearth. If we can look past ourselves, we light up inside and can do the same for others with our infectious, passionate verve for life. As Thomas Jefferson said, "A candle loses nothing of itself when lighting other candles." Let us be so full of passion—which truly enhances performance—that it ignites the hearts of all of those people whose lives we touch. The feelings of accomplishment and satisfaction derived when one helps another human being are beyond measure.

I have always been a firm believer that if you don't like what you do, don't do it. Do something else. Find something to inspire you and spend your time and energy on that.

People often ask athletes, "When will you retire from your sport?" And all great athletes and champions seem to reply in about the same way: "I'll retire when I don't think my next performance will be my best."

If you don't believe your next performance will be your best or you won't try your hardest to accomplish the task set in front of you, then it's time for a change.

Passion will beat down the negative demons, the self-doubt, and the lack of confidence that keep us from achieving great things in our lives.

"We begin as dust and we end as dust. It is what we do in between that really counts."

It is this philosophy that will help us leave a positive legacy for generations to come.

CHAPTER SIX
"PEOPLE"

"The best way to succeed at anything, whether in the classroom or on the job or on the field of competition, is by dedicating one's efforts to special people and by doing everything for everyone else but one's self."

This message is clear: Go out every day and dedicate your actions to others.

Dedicate them to a sick aunt, to grandparents who have passed away, to a little child, or a spouse who helps you through all those difficult moments.

Dedicate them to those in your family who have helped you. They deserve your every act of kindness and thoughtfulness. And don't forget the biggest friend of all, the friend in heaven who catches us when we fall.

Every day of my life is spent dedicating my efforts to special people: my wife, my daughter, my relatives, my friends and students, and the audiences who hear me speak. I give all of them a little piece of myself each day and it makes me a stronger person.

When we place our focus on others rather than ourselves, we make a significant positive impact on mankind that lasts long after we are gone.

"When we put others first, our efforts will be crowned with success."

I love and respect the many other people in my life. Because I do so, I am richly rewarded.

My love and dedication begins at home. My wife, Dianne, and I have a very special relationship as we work together as a team in helping people to build better lives.

My daughter, Sara, has given me the strength to strive to improve myself each day. I was in the hospital room at the moment of her birth, and never felt so much love as I did that day and have felt every day since.

Truly, putting others first enhances performance and

adds significance and indefinable dimension to our lives. When we do so, we are awarded those invisible gold medals.

> **"The human body is simply a container. These containers come in all different sizes, colors and shapes. Some have no hair. Some are old. Some are missing parts. The essence of a human being lies inside the container. The indomitable human spirit is boundless and often untapped. Its potential is equal in everyone."**

I met my wife while I was vacationing with friends in Virginia. Dianne worked at the spa we were visiting and showed me around the facility. The first thing I noticed about her was her voice—soft, Southern, and pleasant to listen to. Although I couldn't really see her, my friends told me she was very attractive, with big brown eyes and a beautiful smile. I could tell she was in good shape because, when I touched her arms, they were slender and firm. She had soft hands with long tapered fingernails and her perfume smelled great.

From the beginning I thought her manner was wonderful—friendly and attentive but very professional. When it came to women, I still had my emotional guard up. I had gone through a painful divorce several years before and I didn't want to get involved with anyone. Yet I couldn't help being drawn to this sensitive woman.

I had just gotten a cane and was still getting used to it, so I let Dianne guide me around the spa to show me the various equipment. Even though the cane was supposed to make me self-sufficient, I was enjoying having Dianne take my arm and walk me around. I just folded up my cane, pretending just this once that it wasn't there.

As the tour ended, I can still remember hearing an Elvis Presley tune that was playing in the background: "I Can't Help Falling in Love With You." Subconsciously I might have been hoping that this was predicting the future.

I had originally come down to Virginia just to get away and hang out with the guys. However, I found myself wanting to spend more time with Dianne than with my friends. In the short time I had spent talking with her and having her so close to me, I realized how much I had missed being close to a woman.

I asked Dianne for a date and she accepted. We had a wonderful time just talking and laughing and getting to know each other. We found out we had several things in common, including difficult first marriages. While mine had ended in divorce, Dianne was still married but legally separated with custody of her three kids.

At the end of the evening, when we hugged each other and kissed good night, it really felt special. Having such an enjoyable time with a nice woman made me feel better about women in general. Because I thought Dianne was so special, I think I started to once again respect other women as well. Perhaps I was just realigning myself with my moral beliefs. Finding Dianne seemed like a reward. Because I had begun to act more like a man is supposed to act, all of a sudden, there she was, right in front of me.

There was a period of time, after my divorce and before I met Dianne, when I did not treat women well. I didn't feel good about myself and I used my self-pity as an excuse to treat the women I dated poorly. I had just recently decided to change my ways, to become more of a Christian and act accordingly.

I called Dianne the next day. "Have you ever been on a blind date?" I asked her. "Of course," she replied. "No, I mean a real blind date, you know, with a date who was actually blind?" She laughed at that and said she'd love to go out with me again.

We had a great time. By the end of the evening, I thought even more of her.

The next day, my friends and I made a group trip to a lake. We invited Dianne along. We had even more fun together. I sensed she was beginning to care for me, and I her, but I had doubts. Did I really want to get involved with someone who had three kids and lived 400 miles away?

Of course, the easiest, most sensible thing to do was to just get out of there and avoid getting emotionally involved. I had only recently begun to bounce back from that divorce and had made my mind up not to get involved. But I was magnetically being drawn into this relationship.

We were all set to leave for New Jersey at 6:30 on Monday morning. I had said my final good-byes to Dianne the night before and was trying to not think about her too much:

Moments before we were to leave, I heard Dianne's van pull up. I was just piling the last piece of luggage into the trunk. She walked up to me, tears streaming down her cheeks, and handed me a card. I was deeply touched because she was so sincere. She was crying and hugging me, holding on to me for all she was worth.

I kept thinking of the movie *Casablanca* where Humphrey Bogart's Rick was saying good-bye to Ingrid

Bergman's Ilsa as she was boarding the airplane to leave him behind in Morocco. This seemed to be my personal *Casablanca.* I was saying good-bye and wondering if I would ever see Dianne again.

Deep down I knew that if I stayed around this lady much longer, I'd fall for her.

I felt tears begin to well up inside me as well which surprised me. I thought I was as cold as a stone and could never feel this way about anyone. I took her card and told her I would have someone read it to me on the way home.

We finally said good-bye and I gave her my phone number. "Give me a call. Maybe we can get together some-time," I told her.

As we headed out, my heart was fluttering. I just didn't know what to do. I thought that with her being so far away, I'd probably never see her again.

In the car, my buddy, Alex, who had known me since college where he was my fraternity brother, said something that caught my attention.

"You know, Rich, there's something special about Dianne. It seemed like you two really clicked. She had a twinkle in her eye when she was around you. I think she might have been falling for you."

I knew Alex was probably right. I knew how strongly I felt about her, but I couldn't help but feel frightened about entering a new relationship.

In the next two weeks after I returned home I went on a couple of dates, but I couldn't get Dianne off my mind.

I finally made a phone call to Virginia. It was great to hear her voice and she said she was glad to hear from me. We had a good conversation and I could tell that I missed being with her. Even so, I tried to tell myself to forget her.

Several days passed after that call. Then, one night just as I was about to fall asleep, the phone rang.

"Rich, is that invitation to come up north still on?" she asked with that sweet Southern accent melting me away. "When can I come up and visit you?"

Well, I'm no Humphrey Bogart. My old stone heart just crumbled into dust. I had been planning to go down to the Jersey Shore with my friends and invited her to come along. I would show her New York City and then take her down to the beach.

When Alex drove me to the airport he was grinning from ear to ear. "What did I tell you, Rich? I knew there was some magic there between you and Dianne."

I couldn't deny it.

Although I was excited to see Dianne again, there was something bothering me. I told her we needed to talk.

I was concerned that she was still married. She protested that she was legally separated, but that wasn't good enough for me. I tried to talk her into going back with her husband for the sake of her children. She was totally opposed to it. She said the marriage had run its course. She didn't love her husband any more.

I told her I wanted her to be happy and successful and would help her in any way I could. I was trying to dissuade her from becoming involved with me.

"Why do you want me?" I asked. "I'm a school teacher, I don't have much money and I'm handicapped. You would have to do special things for a blind person. You really don't want to get serious with me," I argued. "Go find someone who can give you the comfortable lifestyle you deserve. You're too good for someone like me."

Dianne's the kind of person who would never ask for anything. She is proud but stubborn in her own loving, feminine way.

"I've dated guys who had a lot of money before. I'm just not interested in them," she said. "Rich, I'm only interested in you."

I'll never know why she felt that way about me. But I am thankful every day that Dianne is in my life. And I thank her every day by dedicating something to her.

When my friend, Alex, and I were younger, a girl's looks meant everything. We put together a list of the top 10 attributes of a desirable female and beauty was always Number One on the list. Now good looks are nowhere near the top.

Honesty, integrity, loyalty, kindness, family ties, belief in God, strong convictions, fidelity, intimacy, sense of humor. All of those qualities take precedence over looks.

Dianne came up big in every attribute. She had the kind of beauty that is true and lasting.

When you have someone else to live for, life has much more meaning in all ways. Finding Dianne at this time in my life was ironic. When I had my sight, I looked for love everywhere and never found it. When I went blind, she was placed right in my arms.

Her sweet voice, that soft touch, the way she felt snug against me when I hugged her—how good it felt to enjoy these precious moments together.

She inspired and energized me on in all ways because she really loved ME! She also had a strong faith in God, which made our relationship even stronger. This was really too good to be true. My friend Alex had turned out to be a soothsayer.

Dianne and I carried on a long distance relationship for the next year until I found her a job in New Jersey. Since her older children, Sonja and Joey, wanted to stay in Virginia, Dianne moved to New Jersey with her younger son, Seth.

We spent four years together before I felt the time was right to ask her to marry me. I had just won a gold medal in the discus in the Paralympics in Seoul, South Korea, and had received an important athletic award.

I took Dianne to an elegant restaurant ostensibly to celebrate my triumphs. I ordered a bottle of champagne and made a toast.

"Dianne, this is to celebrate my gold medal, my world record, my being named Blind Athlete of the Year."

Then, as nonchalantly as possible, I said, "Oh, by the way, this is for you." I took an engagement ring from out of my pocket and I presented it to her. She couldn't believe her eyes and began to cry.

A little later, the band let me sing a song to my new fiancee. I dedicated "I Can't Help Falling in Love With You" to my future wife.

We were married several months later, on April 16, 1989.

We received a wonderful wedding present from above when we found out that our baby's life began on our honeymoon. Not only was I the luckiest man on the face of the earth to have married Dianne, but in nine months, I would have a beautiful child to call my own!

The baby was due just after Christmastime. On Sunday, January 14, 1990, Dianne woke me at 6:30 a.m. It was time to take her to the hospital.

I called to Seth to wake him up. "Seth, you're going to be a big brother today." He jumped out of bed. He was hoping and praying for a little sister. "We have to be happy with a sister or brother," I told him.

I was in the delivery room, wearing a surgical mask and hospital gown when the baby arrived.

"It has beautiful dark curly hair," said the nurse. "It's a girl!"

As I cut the umbilical cord, hundreds of thoughts raced through my mind. I thought about this little baby girl sitting on my knee. I thought about pigtails and ponytails. I thought about patent leather shoes, her carrying a little pocketbook and running up and greeting Daddy when he got home from work. I thought about the day I'd be walking her down the aisle at her wedding with the song "Daddy's Little Girl" in the background.

I couldn't have been any happier. I was again blessed and unbelievably fortunate. A father can kiss and love and hug a baby girl all of his life. She would always be Daddy's little girl and I could love her forever.

We named her Sara Elizabeth. Sara is a traditional name in Dianne's family. Dianne's proper name is Sara Dianne, and her mother and both of her great-grandmothers were Saras. Elizabeth would be for my mother's mother, a sweet lady who had passed away a few years earlier. We loved the name because it honored both of our family heritages.

As they placed her in my arms, tears welled up in my eyes. My life was now complete. I felt a wholeness, a fulfillment. What a wonderful gift from heaven I had in my hands. My little girl.

Sara's birth also gave me a newfound significance in my teaching career. I suddenly realized the children in my classroom were as important to their parents as my little girl was to me. From that day forward, I have brought to my classroom the feeling that I am teaching a classroom full of Saras. That is the intensity of effort they deserve and I want to give, the same effort I would give to my flesh and blood.

Two years later, I was pursuing another gold medal. This one was especially important to me, because I wanted to dedicate it to my family, my wife and daughter, to earn it as a family man.

I was competing for the United States Disabled Sports Team in Barcelona, Spain, at the 1992 Paralympics—the Olympics for the Disabled. A standing-room-only crowd of 55,000 filled the Olympic Stadium where just weeks before the 1992 Olympics had been staged. The United States had dominated several events with such talented athletes as Carl Lewis, Jackie Joyner Kersee, and the "Dream Team" basketball squad of Michael Jordan, Larry Bird and Magic Johnson.

I would be seeking my final international gold medal, and at age 41, I was the oldest competitor in the javelin.

In the preliminary javelin exhibition, four days

before the actual Paralympic event, I captured first place. It meant nothing other than to establish me as the favorite. Still, when the exhibition medals were awarded that day, I got very emotional as I stood on the victory platform listening to the anthem of the United States played in a virtually empty stadium.

I thought of how my wife, Dianne, and two-year-old daughter, Sara, had been denied the opportunity to witness this awards ceremony. They had walked three miles to the stadium only to be turned away. Dianne could not convince an overzealous security guard of her identity.

Four days later, I returned to the same field to compete in the real event. As the parade of athletes passed by the reviewing stand, the crowd began to cheer wildly. Spain had a viable competitor of its own, 18-year-old Jorge Mendoza, a blind student with two glass eyes who had set his country's national record in the javelin.

Through the crowd noise, my ears picked up on a child's voice that kept saying, "Daddy, Daddy." It was hard to believe, but I was sure I had heard the voice of my daughter in the crowd.

When I heard it again, I turned to my coach, John Kernan, and said, "John, today is going to be my day. I can hear my baby daughter yelling for me."

"Rich, that's impossible," the coach replied.

I knew what I had heard. I pointed to the spot where I heard the voice coming from. Kernan's gaze followed my fingertips. There, in the second deck of the stadium, Kernan saw Dianne and Sara sitting in their seats.

"Rich, how did you do that?" Kernan wanted to know.

"Coach, I don't know. I can't explain," I answered.

With that inspiration, I succeeded in making some solid throws and established myself in first place, only one throw away from my gold medal. The fate of the meet rested on the final throw of Spain's Mendoza, who had never achieved a distance of 43 meters in the javelin. He needed to better that to beat me.

I listened to Mendoza's footsteps as he charged down the runway and then I heard a groan as he let fly. Instantly, I heard the most deafening sound I have ever heard, that of a crowd of 55,000 rising together as it witnessed a surprise victory.

Mendoza had pulled off a unbelievable feat. He set a world Paralympics record of 44.78 meters on his final throw. What a storybook ending for him.

I embraced Mendoza on the victory stand as he was applauded by his countrymen and the Queen of Spain. It was an unforgettable moment for the Spanish, who had not fared well in the Olympic Games, but who now had a true national hero to call their own.

I had known what it was like to win a gold medal for my country. Even though I had to settle for the silver, I was proud and happy at the turn of events.

My coach looked at me in wonder. "Rich, how can you be so happy?" he asked.

"Coach, I've been there before. I know that feeling. This time, someone else gets to have their place in the sun.

"I had my own miracle today, hearing my daughter's voice through a full stadium crowd. I'll take that over a gold medal any day."

As evidenced throughout this chapter, it is only when we complete our jigsaw puzzle of life, fitting together those pieces which represent the important people in our lives, that our purpose comes into focus.

When we know our friends and family are watching us, rooting for us, depending on us, the adrenaline surge and flow throughout our bodies is beyond comprehension. People are what give importance to our performance, a significance that always enhances the performance of champions.

> **"Adrenaline is known as the flight or fight hormone. Those who lack confidence retreat. Champions rise to the occasion and score that personal touchdown just as the final gun goes off."**

Champions are the people who make adrenaline work for them. It's something that can't be coached, but it can be taught by setting an example. When someone faces adversity and rises to the challenge, they earn their reputation as a champion.

When the world says, "You can't," champions say, "Watch me." When we think of all the people we perform in front of, at home, in the workplace, or in competition, nothing makes us strive harder to accomplish our goals than when the oddsmakers say it can't be done. We are here to teach that "world" a valuable lesson, that in life there no overachievers, only underestimators; and that champions move mountains, and if those mountains won't move, they'll drill right through them, because what they want is on the other side.

When we achieve our goals in front of our audiences in life—friends, family, colleagues, even strangers—the feeling of accomplishment and pride is overwhelming. And maybe, just maybe, those who watch us will draw inspiration from our feats to help them on their own life's journey and as they travel through adversity toward success.

Champions realize they can leave a legacy for others to follow by doing things for others. This legacy establishes that doing for one's self pales in comparison to the efforts of those who accomplish great things that influence the lives of countless others.

I have a wife, my faithful companion who loves me, an extended family and step-family who care about me, a little daughter who looks up to me, students who want to learn from me, and audiences who look for inspiration from me as a motivational speaker. All of those people help elevate me to a level of performance that supersedes any level I could have ever attained if I did it just for me.

People truly enhance performance, for without people, there are no performances at all.

CHAPTER SEVEN
"PRAYER"

*"If you truly believe,
you will truly achieve."*

Each and every one of us has problems, our own personal Goliaths we must conquer every day. We can learn a lot from that famous biblical story.

They said David didn't have a chance against his Goliath. He had just five stones to champion his cause and turn the doubters into believers. David's first stone was faith. Faith breeds confidence, confidence breeds faith, and confidence and faith together breed success.

The second stone was courage. When we come up against a wall, we must have the courage to knock it down. And if we can't knock it down, then we must go over or under or around it.

The third stone was obedience, following the rules of life. When we listen to and learn from others, we benefit greatly from the collective wisdom and knowledge of many.

Preparation was the fourth stone. When we prepare for every day with the goal in mind to make tomorrow better, it will be. We must learn all there is to know about what makes us happy, and know that we can always learn more. Our never-ending thirst for knowledge will help us be adaptive, creative and prepared.

The fifth stone was action, putting words into action and walking the talk. We must turn our plans into actions, for actions speak louder than words. Actions are how we are measured. Thought without action is an unfinished sentence.

Faith. Courage. Obedience. Preparation. Action. Just as they helped David, these five attributes will also help us overcome our own obstacles and enhance our performance.

There is one other weapon that David used, perhaps his most important of all. That weapon is prayer.

Prayer is the most powerful tool to enhance performance. In fact, the power of prayer is greater than all of the other performance enhancers already in your toolbox--combined! With prayer, mountains can be moved figuratively and literally. In my life, prayer has taken me to a new level of understanding and into some extraordinary moments.

The power of prayer is undeniable. Prayer can help a person soar to new heights, achieve impossible dreams, attain peak performance.

Because I went blind before I met Dianne, I didn't know what my wife and daughter looked like. I began to wish that I could just have one brief glimpse of them.

I prayed about seeing my wife and daughter, not out of selfishness but out of love. To carry their image inside my heart and mind would mean so much to me.

At this point in my life, I had everything going for me. I was teaching, coaching, still performing well as an athlete and accelerating as a professional speaker. I was happy and fulfilled, but there was one tiny little piece of my life that I would change if I could: I would have given anything to see what my wife and daughter looked like.

During one of my speeches, a little 9-year-old girl posed a question to me that struck me right in the heart.

"Mr. Ruffalo, how can you be so happy when you've never seen your wife and daughter?"

She had managed to zero in on that one thing in my life that I wanted to change. I kept praying, hoping for a miracle.

Believe me, miracles can happen to anybody. They happen to people every day in every walk of life and they are one of the reasons that life can be so exciting and rewarding.

My prayer was, "If I could see them just once, I would be fulfilled on earth. I'm happy now, but I would be so thankful if I could just have those two little pieces in my jigsaw puzzle of fulfillment, seeing my wife and daughter."

It was 1990. I had been stone blind, totally blind since 1984. I had just come home from work, and as I opened the door to our house on that memorable day, a day I will never forget, it was as if someone had turned on a television set. I could see! My wife knows that I joke around a lot, so at first she didn't really believe that I was actually seeing her. When I described every bit of her clothing and jewelry and what colors they were, she realized what was happening. Her eyes got very wide and her jaw dropped.

Then I looked to my right, I saw my six-month-old daughter sitting there on the floor wearing her little outfit and white booties and playing with her toys. I looked at them and drank it all in during my moment of illumination that lasted about 10 seconds.

I was very thankful for this wonderful gift. I've never seen them since but I have all I need to make me happy. My heart and soul experienced a sense of peace and understanding that I cannot put into words. A calm came over my whole being which has enhanced my life ever since.

For those of you who have lost someone dear to you and wondered why, or witnessed the suffering of a loved one who was sick, I'm sure you'll be able to relate to another incident that occurred in my life. It was a revelation that convinced me about the reality of an eternal afterlife.

At the age of 92, my grandmother died in my mother's arms of an apparent heart attack. My mother has always worried and wondered if Grandma felt pain when she died.

While my mother held her, the paramedics worked on this poor elderly women to give her CPR. It's a brutal kind of effort to try to revive someone with the defibrillation pads and extreme pressure that is placed on the chest.

My mother told me how she wondered if, at the end, her mother was in pain from the procedures performed in trying to revive her. I related the story to Dianne one night before we went to sleep.

That night, I was awakened by my grandmother's voice.

"Richie!" she called with her Italian-American accent. "Richie!"

I was shocked and awoke with a start. I sat up in bed and figured I had been having a very vivid dream. I slapped myself to make sure.

Then I heard her again. "Rich! It's me, Grandma."

Now my hair was standing up on end. Chills ran up and down my spine. I tried to wake up my wife, but I'm not sure she was supposed to wake up. My whole body was trembling. I had heard about experiences like this, but now I was witnessing it firsthand. I started to pull the hair out of my legs to make sure I wasn't dreaming. I wasn't. I was wide awake.

Grandma was still speaking to me. I saw a crystal clear picture of her face right over the spot in my mother's kitchen where she passed away. It looked like a window inside a television set. Grandma had a beautiful smile on her face. She was surrounded by a radiant and warm bright white light.

"Tell your mother I'm all right. I'm in heaven. And I'm glad you're happy now. "

My grandmother had been alive when I went through a difficult first marriage and subsequent divorce. She had met my first wife, but not Dianne. When she said, "I'm glad you're happy now," I'm sure she was referring to my new life with Dianne.

She turned to me over her shoulder and said, "I've got to go."

I asked, "Grandma, can you save a place for me?" She said, "All right." And then she said what she always said when she would leave: "Regards to everybody."

That was it. The vision slowly dissipated.

My grandmother came to me with a message to awe others. I will be speaking to a lot of people during my lifetime, and I'm here to share this message: If you open your heart and follow the right path, you will reach your finish line and rejoice in victory with those who passed before you.

Don't look at your departed loved ones as though they're gone forever. Think of them as having finished the race before you did, and that they are waiting to rejoice eternally with you.

I've shared that message with so many people at wakes and Masses and church services for friends and relatives who have died. When I whisper that story in their ear, the response is always the same: They feel a release of tension which is replaced by peace and acceptance.

I know I'm not the only one who has had such incredible experiences. If all of us who have been touched in this way stand up and share those revelations, more people will believe. More people will be inspired to strive higher in their lives.

The power of prayer is incalculable and indefinable. Throughout history, what was considered impossible has come true with prayer. It is the most powerful tool at our disposal. Unfortunately, although it is there for all of us, some people choose to believe it doesn't exist. What a shame! It can help us move those mountains.

In your journey through this book, I've attempted to outline some of the "power tools" you can place in your personal toolbox to help you achieve what you may have previously thought was impossible.

From plummet to pride, pressure, purpose, passion, people and especially prayer, the top three-percenters we so often read about—those who succeed in athletics, in the workplace, in every area of life—possess many of these tools. It is my belief, and hopefully yours, that if you attain several of these performance enhancers, you will achieve success. To maximize your life's journey and take it as far as it can possibly go, continue to add more of these weapons to your arsenal of excellence until you possess them all.

Keep on adding more "P.E.P." to your life, and when you do, sharpen it, hone it and improve upon it to further enhance your peak performance. It can help you to realize your dreams and build legacies that will last forever.

EPILOGUE

EDITOR'S NOTE: Rich Ruffalo feels that his experience in Berlin, Germany, during the Paralympic World Championships in 1994 illustrates perfectly each one of the seven "P's" in P.E.P.

The date was July 31, 1994. The place was Berlin's Olympic Stadium, the same arena in which American Jesse Owens, competing in the 1936 Olympics, triumphed over hatred and racism.

When Rich Ruffalo, accompanied by his coach, John Kernan, walked from the subway, known as the underground in Germany, up a long winding path to the Stadium, this preyed on his mind. There was much significance to this day.

Rich had been in Germany for 15 days preparing for the final event of the International Paralympic World Championships for track and field. It had been a disappointing and harrowing two weeks for Rich.

The United States Blind Athletes Team had arrived in Berlin on July 17th for four days of training for the Games, which were to be held July 22nd to the 31st. On the first day of practice Rich had been reluctant to run sprints during the practice as instructed by the head coach John Kernan. It simply was not part of Rich's training regimen. At 42 years of age, Rich was careful not to overextend the use of leg muscles which were so vital in the throwing events.

(PLUMMET) Coach Kernan kept insisting that Rich sprint with the rest of the throwers on the team. Not wanting to alienate his teammates or appear insubordinate, Rich acquiesced. Only 10 steps into the sprint, Rich felt a searing pain in his right hamstring. He stopped short and fell to the ground, his face buried in the grass, his fist punching the ground. He knew he should have listened to his own instincts.

Tears of frustration burned his face. His sponsors had raised the funds to bring Rich, his wife, Dianne, and daughter, Sara, to the Games and now he might not even be able to compete.

He was taken to the physical therapy tent, and with each step, he felt a grabbing pull of his hamstring. Out of anger and frustration, he picked up a water bottle and threw it away disgustedly, hearing it explode some 50 yards away. The therapists told him he had pulled the hamstring, possibly severely, and if he rigorously followed a rehabilitation program, there was an outside chance he might be able to compete five days later in the discus event. Rich worried about how effectively he would be able to throw the discus since the legs were so vitally important to that event.

Rich knew Coach Kernan was upset for coaxing him into running that sprint that had left him injured. After discussing what could not be changed, the men decided to work together to get Rich as healthy as possible as quickly as possible.

Kernan, a short, wiry distance runner and head track coach at Adams State University in Alamosa, Colorado, was a little Napoleon to his blind athletes. He was physically and emotionally dedicated to whipping his big field athletes into shape. By the conclusion of each track meet, his great intensity and desire to win left him as worn out as his athletes. The athletes respected him and felt an affection for him. Rich had given him the nickname "Special K" and soon all the athletes called him that.

The next day, July 19th, still walking gingerly, Rich met the team outside the hotel to wait for a bus. The athletes were on their way to the stadium where team photographs would be taken. The bus was late, and after waiting several minutes, the athletes were told to sit down.

The Hotel Berlin, where they were staying, was a beautiful hotel with a facade that consisted of glass panels. The athletes were assisted to their seats in front of this glass wall. Rich was the last to be seated. Due to his sore hamstring, Rich settled down slowly, putting his hand on a glass panel to support his descent. Just as he reached the ground and let out a sigh, he heard a popping noise, and then felt something hot and searing in his back.

The glass panel Rich was leaning against had shattered and a chard of glass the size of a large icicle stabbed the burly athlete in the back. Although he remained calm, Rich was stunned by this second dose of bad luck in two days.

They whisked Rich back inside for treatment of the injury. As the physician and his aide removed Rich's Team USA jacket, the doctor noticed that the tank-top shirt Rich was wearing was ripped, and there was a five-inch gash in his back. Although Rich was bleeding profusely, the stab wound proved miraculously to be superficial and no muscles were torn. The wound was not stitched closed, but held together by a series of six butterfly bandages.

The doctor and his assistant inspected Rich's Team USA jacket, which was made of an all-weather-type material. The jacket itself showed no tear at all, while underneath the jacket, Rich's shirt and skin had been ripped open. It made no sense. It was an inexplicable occurrence, a one in a million.

Fortunately for Rich and the team, the jacket had acted as a shield against what might have been a very serious injury, one that certainly would have removed Rich from all competition.

As the week progressed, his back seemed to heal nicely, and the injury became insignificant to the throwing motion that Rich would use in tossing the javelin.

Rich followed the doctor's and coach's rehab regimen precisely so that he could put forth his best effort in the discus. Unfortunately, every time he practiced, a shooting pain went through his right leg as he exploded through his throw. Despite that, as the United States' best hope and a returning bronze medalist from 1992 in the discus in Barcelona, Spain, Rich decided to give it a try.

It was not in the cards that day. Despite a valiant effort that put him in third place with one throw to go, a position he felt was as good as he could achieve coming into these Games, a new entrant, a thrower from Byelorussia eclipsed Rich's distance and secured the bronze medal, dropping Rich into a final fourth place position.

Under the circumstances, Rich felt comfortable with his performance and was looking forward to the shot put and the javelin, his two best events. Both were scheduled to be held on July 31st, the shot put in the morning and the javelin in the afternoon, which would close out the Games. Performing in both events on the same day would take a tremendous amount of stamina. On the positive side, however, with both scheduled on the last day of competition, Rich had eight full days to ready himself and heal his injured hamstring.

Over the next few days, Rich walked briskly each day, working to lengthen his stride. He iced his hamstring before and after every workout and subjected himself to several painful massages each day to relieve the spasms and increase the blood flow. He went so far as to sleep with an ice bag wrapped around his leg.

Rich's work ethic paid off. The brisk walk became a slow laborious jog followed by extensive stretching. After three days of this regimen and five days before the competition, Rich went out to the practice field to try throwing the shot put.

The field for the shot put was strong. The Spaniard who had won the discus with a world-record performance a few days earlier was on track to break a record in the shot put. Rich's teammate Jim Mastro was competing in the event as well and was thought to be the Spaniard's closest competition.

At the practice field that day, Rich failed to achieve the proper explosion from his injured right leg and his shot put fell dismally short of competition-quality distance. Rich and Coach Kernan discussed the situation, and Rich reluctantly agreed to have the coach withdraw him from the shot put competition so he could devote his full attention to the javelin event in which Rich had his best opportunity for a gold medal.

July 31st finally arrived. Rich had worked hard to overcome his obstacles and put their negative effect behind him. He concentrated on looking forward to the javelin competition which would take place in Olympic Stadium with an anticipated crowd of 40,000 people, the largest of the World championships.

At 109 degrees Fahrenheit, the temperature that day was the hottest recorded in a century, making the long walk from the underground to the stadium even longer. The heat seemed to work to Rich's benefit, though, loosening up the tight muscles in his legs on the uphill walk. He felt like a gladiator going into final battle, knowing there was no turning back.

On the practice field outside the stadium, Rich had an assistant coach knead his leg muscles. He refused to take any warm-up throws since he knew he might have only one throw in him before the hamstring muscle would give way. Instead, Rich just relaxed on the ground, stretching and sipping water from a bottle in the overbearing heat.

His wife and daughter surprised him by coming to the practice area to offer their support on their way to the stadium. Rich was amazed that they had even found him since he was lying low in a remote corner of the huge field.

(PRESSURE) His four-year-old daughter, Sara, reached over and kissed her father, and said, "Daddy, I want a gold medal today." That made Rich glow with fatherly pride. His wife, Dianne, added, "I know you can do it, Rich."

Rich promised he would give it his best. Just then, Coach Kernan told the javelin competitors it was time to leave the practice field and to make their way through the catacombs of the stadium to the main arena.

(PASSION) They walked through the entrance platform adorned with six huge stone tablets, three on each wall. One set that faced the field commemorated the XI Olympic Games which took place in 1936. Those were the Games in which Hitler yearned to prove that his "pure Germans," the Aryans, were the best in the world. Ironically, it was a black athlete, American Jesse Owens, who dominated the Games by winning four gold medals.

When Owens was on the highest platform, accepting his final medal as a member of the 4 x 100-yard relay team, Hitler turned his back while the orchestra played the U.S. national anthem. Rich was determined to hear the anthem played for him and to feel what Owens himself had felt.

The blind athletes from every country paraded around the track and moved to the javelin area. At one point during the parade, Rich's keen sense of hearing tuned toward his daughter's voice as she yelled, "C'mon Daddy, you can do it."

Each athlete was allowed two preliminary tosses. Rich attempted them, but only halfheartedly. He was still concerned that he could reinjure that hamstring in his leg.

Coach Kernan watched with some consternation. Since 1992, he was consumed with coaching a world champion in the javelin. He wanted to atone for an over-adjustment he had made on Rich's long throw that was just out-of-bounds and would have given the U.S. the gold two years earlier at the Paralympics in Barcelona.

A ruling change had since come into effect that greatly benefitted the U.S. duo of Kernan and Ruffalo. Coaches were now allowed to give audio cues to blind athletes on their way down the runway during the javelin throw. Since Ruffalo had a tendency to throw to the right, Kernan would stand to the left, allowing Rich to make an adjustment with his head that would help him run straight down the center of the runway, providing a much better opportunity for Rich to keep the   javelin in-bounds.

When Rich learned he would be the last of the six athletes to throw, he relaxed a bit. This gave him a slight advantage because he would know what distance he would have to beat. Still, the adrenaline was already coursing through his body like the old days. He may have seemed calm on the outside, but he was churning on the inside.

The first thrower was the wiry former Soviet who had taken the gold medal in South Korea, leaving Rich in fourth place. This time, however, he represented his true homeland, the liberated Lithuania. He was first up and Rich considered him the class of the competition. Sure enough, his first throw was a beauty, 41.94 meters, a great opening throw that put the pressure on everyone else.

(PRIDE) As Coach Kernan helped Rich into position for his first throw, he offered words of encouragement. Rich knew what he had to do. He couldn't let anybody down by losing, particularly his sponsors who had been so generous and supportive. Rich thought of his parents who would be celebrating their golden anniversary in two years. He thought of how the gold medal had been snatched from his grasp at the last moment in Barcelona.

Kernan went down the line to position himself and begin delivering his audio cue in the cadence of "Rich, Rich, Rich, Rich." That provided Ruffalo with a mental picture of the runway and the direction in which he wanted to run.

Rich grabbed his javelin from the assistant coach. He breathed deeply and focused on the throw, knowing it might be the only one he'd get off. He took a short five-step approach to get a mark, and put himself in the running for a medal. As he took his steps, he remembered to keep his head to the left. He let the javelin go with a wild yell that drew the attention of the crowd.

The sound of their reaction let him know it was a good throw. To regain his balance, Rich hopped three times, but on the final hop, he stepped on the toe line for a foul that nullified the throw. It was a shame because that throw would have placed him solidly in first place at more than 45 meters. Instead it counted for nothing, simply a foul throw. He was reminded of his first national championship in St. Louis, a decade earlier, when the same thing occurred.

The perspiration was pouring off Rich in the heat. But he was wise enough to bring with him a half-dozen water bottles so he could stay hydrated. The Lithuanian had not planned as well. He had nothing to drink, and through an interpreter, he asked Rich for a sip of water. Rich hesitated for an instant, then offered him a drink. The Lithuanian took a quick gulp and handed the bottle back to Rich. This time Rich did not hesitate as he gave it back to his main competitor and, through the interpreter, told him to keep the bottle, adding: "May the best man win." That made the Lithuanian smile, and quickly, each athlete patted the other on the back in the true spirit of sportsmanship. East had truly met West, in Berlin's Olympic Stadium of all places.

The Lithuanian, buoyed by the water, increase his lead on his second throw to 42.28 meters. It was evident he was the man Rich would have to beat, just as he was in South Korea.

Rich, who still needed a mark, threw conservatively and this time threw in-bounds. His distance of 40.58 meters vaulted him into second place.

The Lithuanian could not improve his 42.28 meter

mark on his third throw. Rich strode out confidently to try
and surpass it. His previously-injured hamstring and wounded
back were forgotten in the intensity of the moment. The heat
which was withering the other athletes was helping to loosen
his muscles.

Rich wanted to grab the lead on his third throw. With
his confidence brimming, he burst down the runway, javelin
held high, and let loose with a mighty heave and a yell. The
crowd roared. Then he heard Coach Kernan say, "Darn it.
That was the one. We lost it."

The throw had found its way out-of-bounds to the right
by a mere six inches. It seemed to be a replay of Barcelona.
Kernan came back to tell Rich this throw was about 47.50
meters, which would have been his best in years.

"There's more than one good throw left in me. Re-
lax and take a drink, Coach. I'll take it from here," Rich
told Kernan.

The Lithuanian was apparently wilting in the heat and
was considerably short of his best of 42.28 on his fourth try.
Rich knew that was the mark he had to beat.

Standing on the sidelines as his name was called for
his fourth attempt, Rich thought of many things: that he was
the oldest competitor at age 42, that he had to overcome two
injuries here in Berlin, that the record temperatures could work
against him.

(PEOPLE) In this stadium, in Germany, he thought
of the Holocaust victims, of Hitler's disrespect for Jesse
Owens, and of the millions of innocent lives the maniacal
dictator had terminated. He thought of how none of those
people had a chance to build a legacy.

He thought of all the reasons why he shouldn't be able to win and made those reasons work for him.

(PRAYER) As he grabbed the javelin for his fourth throw, he looked skyward and said, "I have every reason to fail. Let that be my reason for success."

He powered down the runway with all those thoughts running simultaneously in his mind, and let go with an explosive force of energy that seemingly had been lying dormant for years.

He tuned into his coach shouting "Rich, Rich, Rich, Rich," and sent his spear whirring through the thick, humid air. Seconds later, he heard a huge roar, hoping it was for him and not for some other outstanding performance somewhere else in the stadium.

As he turned to walk toward his coach, he thought he had fouled again when Kernan said firmly and fiercely, "Rich, come toward me." As the two men drew closer to one another, Kernan suddenly screamed with joy and wrapped his arms around his burly javelin thrower. "Rich, you did it! You did it!"

The numbers confirmed Kernan's glee. Rich's inspired throw of 45.94 meters had surpassed the Paralympic record set in Barcelona of 44.78 meters by more than a full meter. It was truly an impressive performance for any competitor. It turned out to be a gold-medal throw.

(PURPOSE) Rich Ruffalo had finally taken back the gold. He waved to his little daughter who he heard screaming for him, and ran to the edge of the fence to give Sara and Dianne a hug. His dream of placing a gold medal around his daughter's neck would finally come true.

It was a scene he had pictured in his mind since the day she was born: a medal draped around little Sara's neck, a bouquet of flowers in Dianne's arms, and himself beaming with pride, his arms embracing the two loves of his life.

Rich's rough road to glory had finally been realized with Rich leaving behind a legacy of gold, a legacy that family is gold, bringing forth the message of a brighter tomorrow for the family of man.

Rich Ruffalo is currently training for the Paralympics in Atlanta in 1996 where he hopes his efforts will enable him to present his parents with a gold medal on their 50th wedding anniversary. Regardless of victory or defeat, Rich Ruffalo is dedicated to putting forth a golden effort.

MORE ABOUT RICH RUFFALO

Richard is a biology teacher in the Belleville, N.J. school system and has been an educator since 1973. He coaches discus, shot pur, javelin, track and powerlifting.

His credentials include a BA, with a major in Biology, and an MA degree both from Montclair State University where he was a member of the Science Honor Society. He is also certified as a Principal/Supervisor by the New Jersey Department of Education. In 1985, Rich was named Princeton's Distinguished Secondary School Teacher of the Year.

Richard is an exceptional athlete. He has won four diffcrent world titles in shot put, discus, javelin and powerlifting, 14 international gold medals, set 9 world records, won 32 national titles, set 15 national records, won dozens of gold medals in major meets against sighted competitors and 13 USA Track and Field Masters' State Titles against sighted competitors.

In December 1988, Rich was named Disabled Athlete of the Year for athletic, civic and professional accomplishments by the United States Olympic Committee at the Olympic Training Center in Colorado Springs, Colorado. He was named "Best Lifter" by the Association of Blind Athletes of New Jersey, was a three time winner of the coveted Governor's Cup Award, and won the Victor Award, the academy award of sports, as "Most Inspirational Athlete of 1989." He was inducted into the Italian American Hall of Fame, N.J.

Chapter, and was named National UNICO Amateur Athlete of the Year in 1991. Rich is currently ranked as the top male international blind track and field athlete in the history of the U.S. Disabled Sports Team.

Recently, Rich was named National Spokesperson for the Second Wind Beyond Physical Challenge Foundation sponsored by the National Italian American Sports Hall of Fame. In March of 1994, Rich was inducted into the National Italian American Sports Hall of Fame in Arlington, Illinois. He is the first physically challenged athlete to be recognized and inducted into any national hall of fame. Rich was named Belleville's "Outstanding Citizen of the Year" for 1994, and was one of five inductees from the United States to be selected to enter the National Teachers Hall of Fame in Emporia, Kansas. In 1995, Rich was selected as a finalist in the Disney American Teacher Awards "Teacher of the Year" Program in the athletic coach category. Also, in June 1995, Rich was named Essex County Teacher of the Year. Rich lives in Bloomfield, New Jersey, with his wife Dianne and their daughter Sara.

Note: In November 1995, Rich was named the Outstanding Coach of The Year and the Outstanding Teacher of The Year at the McDonald-Disney American Teacher Awards on national television.

For further information regarding visually impaired or blind person sports participation, I encourage you to call the U.S. Association for Blind Athletes, 719-630-0422.

Major Awards and Honors

Apr. 1985   MONTCLAIR STATE UNIVERSITY
            "Alumni Citation Award"

June 1985   PRINCETON UNIVERSITY
            "Distinguished Secondary School
            Teacher of the Year"

May 1987   BLOOMFIELD, N.J. HALL OF FAME
            Induction

Sept. 1987 BELLEVILLE, N.J. TOWNSHIP
            "Man of the Year"

1988   Selected for "WHO'S WHO" in the East

Jan. 1988   ASSOCIATION FOR BLIND ATHLETES
            OF NEW JERSEY
            "Best Lifter"

Nov. 1988   U. S. OLYMPIC COMMITTEE
            "Blind Athlete of the Year"

Jan. 1989   LIONS CLUB
            "New Jersey Athlete of the Year"

Feb. 1989   U. S. OLYMPIC COMMITTEE
            "House of Delegates Award"

Apr. 1989   GOVERNOR'S COUNCIL For DEPT. OF
            COMMUNITY AFFAIRS
            "Exemplary Recreation Lifestyle Award"

June 1989   VICTOR AWARD (Academy Award of Sports)
            "Inspirational Athlete of the Year"

1990, 1989 GOVERNOR'S CUP AWARD
1987   "New Jersey's Top Blind
                        Track & Field Athlete"

Mar. 1991   NATIONAL ITALIAN AMERICAN SPORTS
                    HALL OF FAME—NEW JERSEY CHAPTER
                    Induction

May 1991   GOVERNOR'S RECOGNITION PROGRAM
                    "Belleville, N.J. Teacher of the Year"

Aug. 1991   NATIONAL UNICO
                    "Amateur Athlete of the Year"

Oct. 1991   E.I.E.S. OF NEW JERSEY
                    "Blind Achiever of the Year"

Nov. 1991   UNITED STATE ORGANIZATION OF
                    DISABLED ATHLETES
                    National Spokesperson

Feb. 1992   NEW JERSEY'S SPORTSWRITERS
                    "New Jersey's Most Courageous Athlete"

Apr. 1992   Selected for Phi Delta Kappa Education
                    Post Graduate Honors Fraternity

Feb. 1993   BELLEVILLE, N.J. HALL OF FAME
                    Induction

Mar. 1994   NATIONAL ITALIAN AMERICAN SPORTS
                    HALL OF FAME, ARLINGTON HEIGHTS, IL.
                    Induction

Apr. 1994   BELLEVILLE, N.J. CONCERNED CITIZENS
                    "Outstanding Citizen of the Year"

June 1994   NATIONAL TEACHERS HALL OF FAME
                      Induction

June 1995   NEW JERSEY STATE DEPARTMENT
                      OF EDUCATION
                      "Essex County Teacher of the Year"

Oct. 1995   STATE DEPARTMENT OF EDUCATION
                      "New Jersey Teacher of the Year 1995"

Nov. 1995   WALT DISNEY AND McDONALD'S
                      AMERICAN TEACHER AWARDS
                      "Outstanding Teacher of the Year"
                      "Outstanding Athletic Coach of the Year "

Oct. 1996   LOUIS BRAILLE AWARD
                      "Associated Services for the Blind"

Oct. 1996   HEALTHY AMERICAN FITNESS LEADER AWARD
                      "U. S. Junior Chamber of Commerce"

Apr. 1997   DISTINGUISHED AMERICAN AWARD
                      "National Football Foundation"
May 1997   Ph.D., Hon.
                      Caldwell College

May 1997   HOMETOWN HERO AWARD AND PROFILE
                      Children's Miracle Network

Sept. 1998   ALWAYS KIDS—HOMETOWN HERO'S
                      "A SALUTE TO EXCELLENCE" AWARD
                      presented by the Quaker Oats Co., broadcast
                      nationally on TNT Network

May 2001   COMMUNITY IMPACT AWARD
                      National Campaign for Victory Over Violence

ATHLETIC ACCOMPLISHMENTS

National and International
(shot put, discus, javelin, powerlifting)

NATIONAL

32 National Titles - USABA

15 National Records - USABA

13 USATF State Masters Championships
    against sighted competitors

Numerous Gold Medals - in major meets against
    sighted competitors - USATF

INTERNATIONAL

26 MEDALS

    14   Gold

    8   Silver

    4   Bronze

    6   World Titles in 4 different events

    9   World Records - IBSA
        (International Blind Sports Association)

COACHING EXPERIENCES

PUBLIC SCHOOL COACHING EXPERIENCES

Myrtle Avenue School, Irvington, N.J.

    1973—Basketball

Belleville Senior High School, Belleville, N.J.

1974-82	Head Cross Country Coach
1974-present	Weight Training Consultant for high school student athletes
1975-84	Head Outdoor Track Coach
1981-85	Winter Track Coach (Club)
1985-present	Assistant Track Coach—outdoor throwing events

OUTSIDE COACHING EXPERIENCES

1989-present	United States Organization for Disabled Athletes (USODA) National Spokesperson/Clinician/National Youth Coach (all physically disabled youths, varied disabilities)
1989	International Pan Am Youth Games—National Coach, International Clinician—shot put, discus, javelin, powerlifting
1990	United States Association for Blind Athletes (USABA)—Head Coach for the World Cup Powerlifting Team for the Blind, won all 3 team trophies for World Cup Championships
1991-present	USABA Elite Athlete/Throwing Coach for Paralympic Training Camps. Paralympic Teams and World Championship Teams

OTHER INVOLVEMENTS

U.S. Olympic Committee Spokesperson for Physically Challenged Athletes

Athletes' Advisory Commission for the International Paralympic Committee—to determine the future of sports for the physically challenged worldwide

1987-present	NJ Tournament of Champions—Spokesperson
1988-present	USABA—Board of Directors
1992-present	APOC—Atlanta Paralympic Organizing Committee Athletes' Advisory Committee/Spokesperson
1993-present	National Italian American Sports Hall of Fame National Spokesperson—Second Wind Foundation—awards scholarships to physically challenged athletes despite ethnicity or national origin

Patent Pending—invention for throwers—Rich Ruffalo's "Tools of Excellence Throwing Kit" for all throwers available next year

RuffStuff

Qty.	Item	Price	Can.Price	Total
	Simply the Best - 3 pk audio	$24.95	$32.95	
	Diamond in the Rough - 6 pk audio	$44.95	$58.95	
	Ruff Road to Glory - 8/90 min. tapes An Autobiography	$49.95	$65.95	
	P.E.P - book	$11.95	$15.95	
	P.E.P. - 2 pk book-on-tape	$19.95	$25.95	
	P.E.P. - 8 pk audio A Spiritual Perspective	$49.95	$65.95	
	How to Enhance Your Performance in Life - video	$19.95	$25.95	
	Tolls for Success in Sales, Business, and Life - video	$19.95	$25.95	
Shipping and Handling Add $3.50 for orders under $20; add $4.00 for orders over $20				
Sales tax (WA state residents only, add 8.6%)				
Total enclosed				

Telephone Orders:
Call 1-800-461-1931
Have your VISA or MasterCard ready.

Fax Orders:
425-398-1380
Fill out this order form and fax.

Postal Orders:
Hara Publishing
P.O. Box 19732
Seattle, WA 98109

E-mail Orders:
harapub@foxinternet.net

Method of Payment:

☐   Check or Money Order

☐   VISA

☐   MasterCard

Expiration Date: _____

Card #: _____

Signature: _____

Name_____

Address_____

City _____ State_____ Zip_____

Phone (   ) _____Fax (   )_____

Quantity discounts are available. • Call (425) 398-3679 for more information.

Thank you for your order!